OUT OF DENMARK

OUT OF DENMARK

ISAK DINESEN/KAREN BLIXEN 1885-1985
AND DANISH WOMEN WRITERS TODAY

Edited by Bodil Wamberg

THE DANISH CULTURAL INSTITUTE
Copenhagen 1985

OUT OF DENMARK

© DET DANSKE SELSKAB 1985

Danish edition entitled *Blixen, Brøgger – og andre danske damer* published by Centrum Publishers, Viby, Denmark, 1985.

Translated from the Danish by *W. Glyn Jones*
Grateful acknowledgement is made for permission to reprint Anne Born's translation of several quotations from *Letters from Africa 1914-1931 by Isak Dinesen*, published © 1981 by the University of Chicago Press.
We also thank Susanna Nied for permission to use extracts from her translation of Inger Christensen's poems *It*.
Lino-cut by Dea Trier Mørch. Courtesy of Vindrose Publishers, Copenhagen.
Photographs by *Rigmor Mydtskov*
Isak Dinesen photographed 1935 by Rie Nissen
Graphic design by *Kitte Fennestad*
Cover portrait of Isak Dinesen based on a photograph by Cecil Beaton, 1959
Copy-edited by *Kate Hegelund*
Printed in Denmark by Special-Trykkeriet Viborg a-s

ISBN 87-7429-058-4

Published by DET DANSKE SELSKAB
The Danish Cultural Institute.
Kultorvet 2, DK-1175 Copenhagen K. Denmark

Distributed in U.S.A. and Canada by
NORDIC BOOKS, P.O. Box 1941, Philadelphia, Pa. 19105

CONTENTS

FOREWORD by *Bodil Wamberg*   7

ISAK DINESEN/KAREN BLIXEN
On Being Oneself, by *Marianne Juhl*   9
Who am I?, by *Thorkild Bjørnvig*   25
The Empty Space Between Art and Church,
by *Aage Henriksen*   45

KIRSTEN THORUP
It's Thorup Today, by *Torben Brostrøm*   59

SUZANNE BRØGGER
You Shouldn't Be Allowed by Put up with It,
by *Jens Kistrup*   77

DORRIT WILLUMSEN
I am only Afraid of Pure Angels, by *Bodil Wamberg*   89

DEA TRIER MØRCH
A Journey in the Soul, by *Erik Vagn Jensen*   103

ELSA GRESS
A Resoundingly Well-integrated Troublemaker,
by *Mogens Knudsen*   121

INGER CHRISTENSEN
and other Women Poets, by *Uffe Harder*   135

THE AUTHORS   157

SELECT BIBLIOGRAPHY   161

INDEX   173

TRANSLATOR'S NOTE

The writer to whom constant reference is made in this book is variously known as Karen Blixen and Isak Dinesen. In order to satisfy both tastes, we have included both forms in the titles and have thereafter followed the preferences of the individual contributors.

Where published texts have already existed these have been incorporated into the main translation. This also applies to Aage Henriksen's text which was used at the Karen Blixen centenary conference in Minneapolis, Minnesota, earlier this year.

FOREWORD

Although this little book will not appear until autumn 1985, it was originally intended to mark the centenary of Karen Blixen's birth on the 17th April. Throughout the year her fellow countrymen have been moved by this occasion to write and lecture on her in an attempt to evaluate her significance for this little country, a significance that still seems to grow greater, the further we come from her life here on earth.

In a paper delivered at a ceremony at Copenhagen University on the actual anniversary, Aage Henriksen quoted a remark which Karen Blixen once made to him: "As long as I live I shall be difficult for you to deal with. But when I am dead you will experience what I experienced when my mother had died and I sat and kept vigil over her. I saw then not only the old woman, but also the young woman and the happy little girl. And then I understood many things I had not understood before".

This is beautifully put, as is everything Karen Blixen said. In her close and natural contact with death she made life vibrate with radiant intensity. But it is not true to say that she is no longer difficult to deal with. Like all great writers and thinkers, she will always be difficult. The price is high for trying to understand her; the whole of one's own existence is at stake when she issues her challenges in her writing. And what she writes always implies an implacable, profoundly disturbing challenge.

In *Out of Denmark* we have chosen to focus on one of the central questions in her work: *Who am I?* Two of the three essays on this theme are written by friends who were close to her while she was alive: Thorkild Bjørnvig and Aage Henriksen. Marianne Juhl joins them with a short essay by the same title and drawing on Karen Blixen's letters from Africa.

Thorkild Bjørnvig answers the question of identity on the basis of the tales and her African memoirs, while Aage Henriksen treats the same problem on an erotic and sensual basis, seeking to define Karen Blixen's universe through a comprehensive understanding of existence. He thereby removes the distinction made in Western civilisation between spirit and matter, which turns love into a narrow and unimaginative moral affair.

Karen Blixen thus stands as the figurehead in this book, but at the same time we also present some other outstanding women writers from the last two decades of literary life in Denmark. The 1960 dividing line of the bibliography (pp. 161-171) is naturally artificial and without literary juristification, and its sole purpose is to limit the scope of the book.

Each of these authors is presented by literary scholars and critics who have been particularly concerned with their work. The contributors have all been free to tackle the job as they have considered most appropriate. Some have laid their main emphasis on the personality creating the myth about the writing, while others have seen it as their task to analyse ideas and views of life. However, the invisible heading over each and every one, whether biographical or analytical, is still: Who am I?

This little group of women authors does not reflect real feminist literature as such, not, that is, in the sense of militant literature. The more highly individualised writing stemming from cultural developments over the last ten years has resulted in the particular characteristics of individual authors coming more and more into their own.

Last but not least, the book seeks to introduce some of the poetry written by Danish women today. Here we have naturally been faced with the fact that it is far more difficult to do justice to poetry than prose in translation, and to ensure that its individual character is not lost. This has been overcome as far as possible by the American translator of Danish poetry, Susanna Nied, the Danish poetry expert Uffe Harder, and the translator of the main text, W. Glyn Jones, Professor of Scandinavian Studies in the University of Newcastle upon Tyne.

Copenhagen, June 1985   *Bodil Wamberg*

ISAK DINESEN/ KAREN BLIXEN

On Being Oneself

by *Marianne Juhl*

KAREN BLIXEN (1885-1962). Married to baron Bror Frederik Blixen-Finecke (1914-
1925). Upon her marriage she went to Africa,
where she ran a coffee farm in Kenya (1914-
1931). Her lack of success and ability as a cof-
fee-planter forced her to return to Denmark.

She became known as the great storyteller
under the pseudonyms of Isak Dinesen and
Pierre Andrézel. Apart from one novel, her
work consists of a large number of short stories, written and published in English and
Danish and then translated into many other
languages.

Honorary Member of The American Academy 1957. Member of The Danish Academy
1960.

Karen Blixen's *Letters from Africa*, written to her family in Denmark over the 17 years she lived on her coffee farm in Kenya, trace a woman's development from the nice, well-brought-up and well-adjusted daughter of an upper middle class family, entering into what promises to be a perfectly traditional marriage, to the liberated and self-assured woman who in 1931 would rather have chosen death by her own hand than live a life in which she was denied the possibility of independent action. It was a radical process that the women of Denmark were two generations in undergoing. As for Karen Blixen, it betokened at the same time a progression from the artistic dreams of youth, hesitantly manifested in a few poems and a few tales and attempts at tales, to the author of the brilliant *Seven Gothic Tales*, which were written in part towards the end of her stay in Africa.

What brought this about? Both personal and external factors played their part. Misfortune and illness overwhelmed Karen Blixen and prevented her from adopting the role and career for which she had been prepared in a general way. Syphilis, divorce and the threat of financial disaster would have made most people succumb or give in. Deep down inside her, Karen Blixen had reserves of strength and determination to keep her going. But it required an unflinching resolve to arrive at the truth before she could reach the fundamental core of personality hidden beneath the many layers deposited by the upbringing which that time and that social background typically inflicted on a young woman.

At a time when many others relax comfortably in a habitual way of life and with an identity long established, Karen Blixen had the courage to rebel against her entire life so far and to look deep into herself in order to discover the outlines of her original personality, to get to know herself.

WHO AM I?

In the night I hear
from silent woods
a cry like: help me,
my God!
I rise, listen,
am unable to sleep.
Who am I?
How do I
look?

The poem is by Holger Drachmann, and Karen Blixen quotes it in a letter to her brother Thomas Dinesen in 1926. At the same time she wishes for him that he may find his own "personality expressed in action". The reason why Karen Blixen gives her brother just this advice in 1926 is that she herself has been battling with the question for the past few months and has for the first time found some answer to the riddle of her own personality. She goes on to comment on the poem:

"I think that he says something real, true, there. In a way this is what one is always searching for in life. By trying to look into oneself one can somehow only glimpse it, or one can see the drawing of, the model of the house or ship that is to be built; in one's work, one's profession, the impression one makes, the relationship one has with the outside world – its people and ideas – one comes to know it, one somehow sees it face to face." (5.8.26)

There is good reason to consider the two principal points of view in the letter: firstly that Karen Blixen regards the question of "Who am I?" to be fundamental in life. In this the artist reveals herself, at least if one is to assume that a powerful need for self-understanding is one of the most essential motive forces in artistic creativity. The other is that she believes that you can only "arrive at a vague impression" of yourself by turning your gaze inwards. If you seriously want to explain yourself you must look at the *work* you are doing and the *impression* you make on others.

THE LOSS OF A ROLE

However, many years were to pass before Karen Blixen managed to formulate a conviction such as this. In her early letters, written between 1914 and 1921, there is no sign of problems centred on identity; nor are there any letters in which she appears to be concerned with her own personality or status. She seems to have settled into a life as the wife of a coffee planter, Bror von Blixen; and although a wife's role in that primitive settlers' environment is far from that of a wife in Denmark, and although she plays an active part in the life of the farm, joining in safaris and so on, she nevertheless does so within the framework of a well-defined role. Despite the fact that Bror von Blixen is responsible for her contracting syphilis and thus makes the first dent in the marriage, Karen Blixen loyally holds on to what she is familiar with and does not ask for a divorce. And although she gradually comes to be viewed as the "difficult" child of the family, she is still the obedient daughter who every week writes long letters home to "My beloved mother" and "Dearest Tommy".

Not until 1921, when the question of a divorce from Bror von Blixen arises – at first in the form of the family's earnest "advice", later as Bror's own express wish – do the introspective letters appear. Karen Blixen may well be right that the question of self-knowledge follows us throughout our lives but for long periods is only latent. When the question intrudes and demands a reply or at least serious consideration, it does so in situations in which personality is put to the test. Either because you are excluded from a familiar and defined role, or because you renounce it of your own volition.

This is what happens to Karen Blixen in 1921. At first her family's interference provokes her to define herself in relation to the Westenholz, i.e. maternal, side of the family. You do not understand me, she writes, I am different from you. And she goes on:

"I feel that Mama and Aunt Bess and the whole of your family, (...) if they care for me at all, do so in a way in spite of my being as I am. They are always trying to change me into something quite different; they do not like the parts of me that I believe to be good." (Autumn 1921)

Especially this last sentence opens the view on a gulf of misery in Karen Blixen's childhood. To bring up a child in such a way that it comes to doubt the value of its own innate being and qualities does irreparable damage both to its self-confidence and its self-understanding. One senses just how the powerful women's regime in Rungsted devastated Karen Blixen's possibility of disovering her own identity and daring to admit to a personality that did not conform to the norm which the age and the surroundings imposed on a woman.

In the next letters Karen Blixen elaborates further on the distance at which she feels herself from her relatives. I am made happy or unhappy by quite other things than you, she writes. I did not make too much of my illness, and I would have made even less of it, had it not been for you. But nothing in the world would make me go back to a time when I had to have dinner at Folehave every Sunday.

She quite consistently maintains this attitude throughout the rest of her letters. She would rather suffer the pains, the obstacles and difficulties that an active life of necessity will bring in its train than be enclosed in the inert idyl and happiness offered by the idle, passive life she knew from her maternal relatives' trio of houses at Rungstedlund, Folehave and Matrup. That Karen Blixen was not alone in this experience of her childhood surroundings is obvious from Thomas Dinesen's attempt to break out. He volunteered for military service during the first world war and later wrote an enthusiastic book *(No Man's Land)* about how wonderful it was to go to war. He did not take part for idealistic or political reasons, but because the war offered excitement and passion and made an absolute demand for personal commitment, for dedicated effort, in contrast to the "colourless little life at home".

KAREN COFFEE CO.

While Karen Blixen lost her role and status as a wife, with all the sense of defeat this must have inflicted on her self-respect as a woman, she gained in independence on the other hand after the divorce from Bror von Blixen by becoming the managing director of the Karen Coffee Co. and taking charge of the running of the farm.

"And I am so very fond of my house and garden and the whole farm; I have the feeling, which one seldom gets at home, that I have created this myself and that it is a part of me (…) that I have become what I was meant to be here, which is perhaps something better than you at home can believe." (23.1.22)

Or, in the words Karen Blixen uses in her letter from 1926 – she can see her own personality expressed in action – what, some fifty years later became known to the women's movement of the 1970s as "realising oneself".

For the next few years the fate of the farm seems to stabilize itself sufficiently for her to believe that the task in which she is now investing her physical and mental powers will continue. The letters now become marked by a sense of optimism and confidence in the future:

"I should like to give all young women two pieces of advice: to have their hair cut short and to learn to drive a car. These two things completely transform one's life. (…) And as nobody wears corsets out here you can really move as a man's equal." (January 1923)

"Incidentally, I think that there is a really fine time ahead for women and that the next hundred years will bring many glorious revelations to them." (2.8.23)

Karen Blixen has clearly settled in her new role as coffee planter and a mixture of queen and mother to her black workers. *Freedom* becomes a key word in her letters from now onwards. The outer framework in her life is now such that she can feel happy, i.e. "freely able to develop her character to the utmost". (19.8.23). Moreover, during these years she is having a love affair with the man who realises her ideal, the English business-man and safari guide Denys Finch Hatton. In this condition of twofold freedom, freedom to "be as I am" and freedom to live with the man whom she deeply loves, the "Who am I?" of doubt and lacking self-confidence is replaced by the self-assured "I am". Her letters are full of views on all manner of circumstances, expressed unhesitatingly and often in conscious opposition to her relatives at home. In every other letter she sings the praises of her African way of life, her *joie de vivre* and her love.

MY STRENGTH HAS GONE

However, this did not last for long. Even by the autumn the earth is shaking beneath her again: the unprofitable farm is once more threatened with closure:

"... Since I received Uncle Aage's letter the scent has gone from the roses and the radiance from the full moon in my life here and I have been feeling much as I imagine Samson felt when they had cut off his hair: my strength has gone." (10.9.23)

The insecurity of the farm as the basis of Karen Blixen's life begins to make her dependence on the other fixed point in her life – Denys Finch Hatton – all the greater. However, in Karen Blixen's own words, Denys Finch Hatton was "uncommittable", not wishing to bind himself in any contractual relationship, but

18

he came and went in Karen Blixen's life as *he* wanted. Throughout the next couple of years the mood in her letters varies sharply. At times she is the happiest person on earth, at others she is
despondent and depressed. And a careful examination reveals
that the violent changes of mood are determined by Denys Finch
Hatton's presence on or absence from the farm:

"Otherwise I am well and have been happier than anyone else on
earth because I have had Denys staying here for a month. (…)
That such a person as Denys does exist, – something I have
indeed guessed at before, but hardly dared to believe, – and that
I have been lucky enough to meet him in this life and been so
close to him, (…) compensates for everything else in the world,
and other things cease to have any significance." (25.9.23)

"I believe that for all time and eternity I am bound to Denys, to
love the ground he walks upon, to be happy beyond words when
he is here, and to suffer worse than death many times when he
leaves." (3.8.24)

These two examples could be supplemented with a couple of
dozen more between now and May 1925, when Karen Blixen
returns to Denmark for the third time since she left for Africa.
She stays at home for eight months, and this time it is very
doubtful indeed whether she can or will return to the farm. At all
events she makes use of her stay to try to make contacts in the
literary world in Denmark, which could seem to indicate that she
is seeking different possibilities for the future. Her Aunt Bess
arranges a meeting with Georg Brandes. He is the leading literary critic of the time, and perhaps Karen Blixen hopes to find
support to realise her old plans for becoming a writer. She also
sends various little things to the poet Ludvig Holstein, now a
publisher's reader with the Gyldendal Publishing House; these
include the marionette comedy *The Revenge of Truth* and the
poem "Moonlight", with the Greek goddess of hunting, Artemis,
as a recurring figure.

Meanwhile, Karen Blixen's considerations finally lead to her

2*

going back to Africa in February 1926. Her first letters after her return make very depressing reading. She is ill and feels "devoid of energy for work and life …" (29.2.26). Denys is on safari. But in March her mood and health are suddenly splendidly restored: "I have had the great joy and happiness of having Denys here for two days". (7.3.26). Karen Blixen is again on her switchback, but this time she plunges wildly into an abyss deeper than she can tolerate.

THE TURNING POINT

Exactly what brings about the decisive new view of herself which becomes the turning point in Karen Blixen's life does not emerge from the letters. It was presumably a combination of various factors. Just before leaving Denmark in 1925 she was told by her solicitor that her divorce had finally gone through. Perhaps that had led her to expect Denys Finch Hatton to enter into a more permanent relationship, but the hope was not fulfilled.

The articles on Africa which she had promised to a Danish newspaper and worked on for the last year refuse to take shape. And *time* is passing: Karen Blixen is now 41 years old. In the winter tale "Heloise", she writes many years later: "It is we, the women in the world, who feel it. Time takes so much from us. And finally it takes everything".

At all events, on the first of April, in a letter to Thomas Dinesen – the most important of all these letters – she starts formulating the understanding she has achieved during the recent months of doubt and despair:

"I must try to write to someone to whom I can speak absolutely frankly and truthfully from my present standpoint, – that is why I am sending you this letter now." (1.4.26)

For the first time she accepts that her life is entirely ruled by her feelings for Denys Finch Hatton; she realises why this is, and finally makes the decision that it *must* not go on like this:

20

"... my whole existence revolves around this relationship as around an axis, (...). But I will not and cannot continue to go on living in this way, with this single element in my life; (...) No, you see, I must *be myself*, be something in myself, have, own something that is really mine, achieve something that is mine and is me, in order to be able to live at all ..." (3.4.26)

This *no* becomes the great and decisive turning point in Karen Blixen's life because at the same time it is her *yes* to herself. It is not a *no* in relation to a man, but a *no* to his being the *entire* content of her life. Here she accords the first priority in life to herself and what she can achieve. The fact that she does not at first feel that she has anything with which to fulfil this potential is not so important. What is significant is that the way is open for her in the coming years to rediscover the greatest force in her personality – her ability to write.

Before Karen Blixen reaches this point, however, there is much to be unravelled and many inhibitions to be removed. She sets about this already in this April letter and proceeds with the task until 1931, when the loss of the farm throws her into such deep water that she is forced to see whether the ability to write can also keep her *afloat*.

FROM LETTERS TO TALES

The difference with her childhood home, which began in 1921, develops now, in 1926, into a total disagreement. What originally held her back was the family's "love" and "kindness". Now she realises that *love of* was too closely related to *power over*, a power which they used in order to rob her of her independence and leave her abilities to lie fallow. *That* realisation makes possible a showdown with her family and later her revolt against the dominant ideal of womanhood of the day.

As she so often does, not least in the tales, Karen Blixen uses a mythical figure as a symbol for a personal set of problems, in this

21

case Lucifer, the angel who rebelled against Paradise and was cast down into his own realm. But she reproaches herself for not having had Lucifer's vision and breaking long ago with the spirit of Paradise:

"I have betrayed my angel Lucifer and sold my soul to the angels in Paradise, and yet I cannot live in it;" (3.4.26)

Later in the letter Karen Blixen emphasises that by Lucifer she does *not* mean anything demonic – so she is not thinking of Lucifer as the Devil – but what lies implicit in the original meaning of the word, the bringer of light:

"I conceive of it as meaning truth, or the search for truth, striving toward the light, a critical attitude, – indeed, what one means by *spirit*. The opposite of settling down believing that what one cares for is and must be best, indeed, settling into the studied calm, satisfaction and uncritical atmosphere of Paradise. And in addition to this: work, – I think I can work longer and get less tired than most people, – a *sense of humor* which is afraid of *nothing*, but has the *courage of its convictions* to make fun of everything, and life, new light, variety."

In several letters written after 1926 and in the essay "Modern Marriage and Other Reflections" from 1923 Karen Blixen touches on her family's rigoristic efforts to create idyl and harmony in their own little isolated circle by suppressing or excluding all irrational forces in life, and then to maintain into the bargain that happiness looks like this and only like this. It is not difficult to understand that in an atmosphere which excluded criticism and denied basic human inclinations, creative activity was impossible:

"I cannot, I cannot *possibly* write anything of the slightest interest without breaking away from Paradise and hurtling down to my own kingdom." (1.4.26)

The letter from April 1926 is full of fears that during the past years she has lost her personality, exhausted her own qualities, and yet at the end there is a tiny ray of hope:

"I know that you think I could write. And I think that I could, if I could come to find myself in circumstances where I could be open to impressions that would help me to be inventive again." (4.6.26)

In the continuation of this letter, which Karen Blixen sends off on the 5th September, that hope has grown:

"… it was a necessity for me to write in this way before I could get started on something else, my marionette plays for instance, which I really must get on with now." (5.9.26)

In the following years Karen Blixen nevertheless still devotes much energy to the farm and her relationship with the blacks, so much so that at first she feels a total loss of identity when the farm has to be sold in 1931. But by then she *has* started writing, and that is what her life is based on from now onwards: expressing her personality in tales and making her way through her writing to an understanding of the question: Who am I?

Marianne Juhl

All quotations translated by Anne Born

ISAK DINESEN/ KAREN BLIXEN

Who am I?

by *Thorkild Bjørnvig*

It was not until late in her life that Isak Dinesen actually formulated the question: "Who am I?" Nevertheless, although not expressed in words, it was quickly implicit in her thinking, and the answers were given at an early stage. Two of them were clearly enunciated for the first time in the marionette comedy, *The Revenge of Truth*, the first version of which was a little play written for the family in 1904. She took it with her to Africa and back and finished it during a visit to Denmark in 1925. It is Amiane, a kind of fairy or witch in the play, who gives the answers. First she says:

"You are one of the ideas of Nature, and they are all wise. The woods where I come from are Nature's as well, they are her deep thoughts, and the cows in the pastures are good and pretty fancies."

However, in her next lines she abruptly changes her theme:

"The truth is that we are all acting in a marionette comedy. – My children, what is more important than anything else in a marionette comedy is to keep the author's ideas clear. To act in a marionette comedy is a true blessing, and now that at long last I have come into one, I will never go out of it again. But you, my fellow actors, keep the author's idea clear. Aye, drive it to its utmost consequence."

A human being is, then, both a marionette and one of Nature's thoughts. Are these two names for the same things? As put in this play, it might seem to be the case, but in reality it is not so, and in Isak Dinesen's subsequent writings it emerges that the two concepts represent two radically different views on human life and behaviour, two distinct perceptions of human identity.

While marionettes are related to an author, normally regarded as a human being, embodied thoughts are an emanation from nature, normally regarded as a non-human being, if, indeed, it is a being at all. However, an author and an artist have something about them of God the Creator, or at least of a godlike being; Isak

Dinesen's poem "The Ballad of My Life" begins: "An artist is the good God –" And Nature as well as the Earth can be felt and experienced as a god or goddess. But God, when conceived as an artist or author, inevitably acquires human, often too human, characteristics and qualities – while Nature and the Earth, when perceived as a god or goddess and as visible reality, preserve, deep down, something unalterable and mysterious. In a letter written to her mother from the farm, Isak Dinesen tells of an earthquake she has experienced. It was only a slight one, but it was the first in her life:

"I was in the bathroom getting ready for bed, and my first thought was that a leopard had somehow or other got into the loft; but when the whole house began to rock I had to think of another explanation. Although it is an unpleasant feeling in itself, there is something almost intoxicating about it when something you have considered lifeless starts to move. You feel as though you must pat the earth and talk to it and say: 'Oh, so you are alive after all, my old Earth'."

Not only we, but also the forests are the deep thoughts of nature, and the cows her good and pretty fancies, says Amiane in *The Revenge of Truth*. Isak Dinesen's favourite twentieth-century poet, Sophus Claussen, has these lines in one of his last poems:

Are you wiser than the tree, the tree deep in the forest,
sensing a pact with created things around, above, below?
Surely the tree in the heart of the forest
can feel the forest's soul.

Don't you think the forest saw you with its silent thousand
branches,
though you thought yourself alone,
with my eye resting on you?
Do you think the tree cannot sense?
Don't you believe the forest thinks?

28

One of the characters in "The Deluge at Norderney" is a young girl named Calypso. In a certain tense situation she is standing with an axe in her hand at the bedside of her boy-loving, woman-hating uncle, intent on killing him because he has denied her existence. It is not casual or vaguely poetical when Isak Dinesen likens the girl to "a limetree in bloom", an image she added to the later Danish version of the story. The tree thinks – an attribute of human beings – while the girl blossoms like a lime-tree – an attribute of trees. For Isak Dinesen the connection between man and the manifestations of nature is essential. The relationship does not imply any disparagement of human beings, but it is indicative, rather, of praise. This attitude is clearer still when applied to the relationship between man and animals, and it is one of the most striking and unchanging elements throughout the entire corpus of her work.

IDENTITY FROM WILD ANIMALS

There are people to whom not only the sight, smell and touch, but the mere existence of animals is an embarrassment and worry – and there are those who cannot imagine a life without animals. In "The Deluge at Norderney" extreme examples of these two types are confronted with each other in the persons of Calypso and her uncle. In her desperate attempt to appear as a boy among the other lovely, seraphic boys in the castle, Calypso has resolved to cut off her breasts. There is in the castle a room which no one ever uses. She goes to it and tries her axe on her little finger – when suddenly, in a long mirror hanging on the wall, she sees a large figure behind her. Turning around, she catches sight of an enormous old painting of fauns and satyrs, nymphs and centaurs. This is the moment when she is saved and fundamentally changed; in a flash she realises her place in the totality of creation, indeed discovers that she has a place in it at all; she realises that the young women in the picture, with figures exactly like hers, are adored and desired by these strange, odd and fabulous creatures. The account of this wondrously joyful experience is a key sequence in the story of Calypso. And it is more than that: here, conceived as a clash between two psychological types in a fantastic tale, we see one of the decisive and fatal divisions in western civilisation. Not a clash between abstract ideas, but between basic sensual experiences. We read:

"She looked with great interest at the satyrs and centaurs. In her lonely existence she had developed a passionate tenderness for animals. To the mind of Count August the existence of the brute creation was an enigma and a tragedy, and there were no animals at Angelshorn. But to the girl they seemed sweeter than human beings, and she was delighted to find that there were people who possessed so many of their characteristics."

At the time when the animals seem "sweeter than human beings" to Calypso, she is in a state of crisis. Though not in the same situation, Isak Dinesen always loved and praised animals, but in Africa she really met *wild* animals for the first time. It was an overwhelming experience. In tones reminiscent of Saint Francis of Assisi's "Canticle to the Sun", indeed a continuation and expansion of it, she writes, in *Shadows on the Grass:*

"Praise be to thee, Lord, for Brother Lion, the which is very calm, with mighty paws, and flows through the flowing grass, red-mouthed, silent, with the roar of the thunder in his chest."

And later she continues:

"Praise be to thee, Lord, for Sister Giraffe, the which is an ambler, full of grace, exceedingly demure and absent-minded, and carries her small head above the grass, with long lashes to her veiled eyes –."

And not only did she feel wild animals as a sublime kind of sisters and brothers – she also saw them as examples. She writes:

"In very old days the elephant, upon the roof of the earth, led an existence deeply satisfying to himself and fit to be set up as an example to the rest of creation: that of being mighty and powerful beyond anyone's attack, attacking no one."

This was, she adds bitterly, in the time before this "manifestation of God was turned into an object of exploitation", because of ivory hunting.

The fundamental reason why wild animals are examples, especially to human beings, is that they conform exactly to God's ideas and become what He means them to be. They do not interfere with God's plan, as human beings, under constraint or of their own volition, all too often do. This is the theme in "Peter and Rosa" from *Winter's Tales*. The fifteen-year-old Peter lives at the home of his uncle, who wants him to be a clergyman. But Peter wants to go to sea. In a conversation at night alone with his uncle's daughter, who is the same age as he, he declares to her that this is what God intends for him, for God has intentions with everything He has created, from stars and trees to beasts and birds; they are examples to be understood and followed. Then he takes a more modest wild animal as a proof and model for his line of reasoning:

"I saw a fox the other day by the brook in the birchwood. He looked at me, and moved his tail a little. I reflected, as I looked back at him, that he does excellently well at being a fox, such as God meant him to be. All that he makes or thinks is just foxlike, there is nothing in him, from his ears to his brush, which God did not wish to be there; he will not interfere with the plan of God."

When a creature on this earth is fulfilling God's plan, identity is no problem. There is no rift, no vacuum, in the limetree, the fox or the elephant to generate this question. But if a human being, perhaps in need, perhaps from a surplus of energy and lust, attempts to achieve the same certainty about his own condition and ability, he has the possibility of proceeding a step further. Not only can he use the wild animal as an example, but he can identify with it. This applies *not* to the tame, domesticated and often confused animal, but to the *wild* animal. In Africa Isak Dinesen, together with her special friends, takes this step. In *Shadows on the Grass* she writes without reservation:

"We registered ourselves with the wild animals, sadly admitting the inadequacy of our return to the community – and to our mortgages – but realising that we could not possibly, not even in order to obtain the highest approval of our surroundings, give up that direct contact with God which we shared with the hippo and the flamingo."

And this applies also to her beloved servant Fahra:

"For Fahra, although posing as a highly respectable majordomo, was a wild animal and nothing in the world would ever stand between him and God."

This was, to Isak Dinesen, one way to realise identity, to answer the question: Who am I? It happened in the real world, in Africa, when she was an affectionate woman, a magnetic centre for friends and squatters, living with all the responsibilities for them and the farm. The developmental course of this insight was first the view that every being is a thought of nature, then an idea of God, and finally a manifestation of God. This was the case with wild animals and a possibility for human beings with the qualities and integrity of the wild animals concealed in their hearts, giving them the potential for direct contact with God and the fulfilment of His plan. Let us now return to *The Revenge of Truth* to examine the other path explored by Isak Dinesen.

IDENTITY FROM THE STORY

"The truth is that we are all acting in a marionette comedy", says Amiane. And finally she adds: "But oh, my fellow players, keep

the author's idea clear. Aye, take it to its utmost consequence."
Then, she implies, you will find your identity, or, in the words of
Isak Dinesen later in her career, you will discover who you are.
But by that time, at the end of her life and with her major works
behind her, living not as a young woman, not as a farmer playing
with the idea, but as a great artist and famous storyteller, she had
replaced the marionette comedy with the story. It happens in
"The Cardinal's First Tale" from Last Tales.

What is the reason for this fascination with the marionette
comedy, which doubtless contains the seeds of her philosophy of
the story? Certainly, there was the sheer delight of playing, but
there was also a kind of desperation. Just as Calypso in her non-
existence in the castle turns to animals, and as Isak Dinesen after
a shooting accident on the farm, her heart heavy with the tragedy, says: "I turned to the animal world from the world of men"
– so she turns to the world of marionettes. Neither the world of
animals nor the world of marionettes was, in her opinion, anything for the kind of people, the class, she had a grudge against,
i.e. the bourgeoisie, the respectable middle classes. Curiously
enough, one of the great poets of the present century, Rainer
Maria Rilke, shares this feeling, and in one of his Duino Elegies,
the fourth, the most desperate and hopeless of them, he clearly
states how much he prefers the marionette, the doll, to the bourgeois, and he explains why:

Who's not sat tense before his own heart's curtain?
Up it would go: the scenery was Parting.
Easy to understand. The well-known garden,
swaying a little. Then appeared the dancer.
Not him! Enough! However light he foots it,
he's just disguised, and turns into a bourgeois,
and passes through the kitchen to his dwelling.
I will not have these half-filled masks!
No, no, rather the doll. That's full.

Because the doll is empty, perfectly empty, it can like the poet be
filled with the breath of inspiration, like the mystic with the

unknown God, like the wise man with insight, and like the dancer with the spirit of the dance. True emptiness is the necessary precondition, and to the doll in Rilke's elegy comes the angel to fill it and move it. And, as the triumphant line then has it: "Angel and doll! Then there's at last a play."

To abandon the half-filled, respectable place and occupation in ordinary life and become a doll, a marionette, in the tragedy or comedy of existence is, to Isak Dinesen, one of the most powerful means of discovering the meaning of life and of realising one's identity. This idea became more and more serious to her, as is reflected in the imperceptible transition from the part in the marionette play to its significance and role in the story.

It will probably be difficult to find an apologia for the story – indeed, almost an apotheosis of it – equal to that which Isak Dinesen wrote in "The Cardinal's First Tale".

A lady in black asks the Cardinal: "Who are you?" To him it is quite clearly a provocative and inspiring question, and he answers it by telling the story of his life. Thereupon he outlines a philosophy of the story which is clearly derived from the modern novel. He calls it "the literature of individuals". What happens to them is occasioned by their own mind and character; as far as it is possible they will fashion their own stories in accordance with their own wills and desires, and perhaps their own piteousness and weakness, and thus arouse the modern reader's sympathy and pity. But this will not be a real story; on the contrary, it will lose its impact and ultimately be dissipated. How different from the original story, the immortal story. This creates and immortalises the hero, no matter what are his own qualities, what is his character or his temperament. There is only one condition: that he or she shall not try to influence their role in the story, even if it is to be tragic and terrible. To the lady, the penitent, this seems scarcely human, but the Cardinal maintains that the story is a divine art and therefore devoid of any irrelevant compassion that could change it – while the modern novel is a human product. He gives some famous instances of classical stories with tragic endings and concludes with these words on the genuine, the divine story:

"– to its human characters there is salvation in nothing else in the universe. If you tell them – your compassionate and accommodating human readers – that they may bring their distress and anguish before any other authority, you will be cruelly deceiving and mocking them. For within our whole universe the story only has authority to answer that cry of heart of its characters, that one cry of heart of each of them: 'Who am I'."

The marionette comedy has an author, and the characters must keep the idea of the author clear. In connection with "The Cardinal's First Tale" it is interesting and significant that there is no indication of an author.

"In the beginning was the story," says the Cardinal. Not an author. Not a creator. There is no word of a possible Divine plan for human beings, for beings at all, and only human beings are important and meaningful in this tale. In view of the multitude of animals in Isak Dinesen's other tales, not to speak of her books on Africa, animals experienced in reality, as images of human characteristics and qualities, and as means to discover one's identity, it is striking and strange that only horses and dogs are mentioned in this tale, as clichés, as devices on a shield or pictures on a playing card. A bowl of goldfish is a comical exception, as conventional as a bird cage. There is not a single reference to a creature of the wild, whether bird or beast.

It is clear that one way of discovering identity – by means of the divine story – excludes the other – that of living according to God's plan, like the wild animals. However, it is difficult to avoid the conclusion that the philosophy of the story is generated by the great, established artist and storyteller, that it springs from this role in her life – and not from that of the farmer, the compassionate woman of flesh and blood, the sister of the lion and the giraffe, who pondered God's plan with her and sought to discover how to realise it.

There is no record or indication that there was a risk of misunderstanding and hubris in the latter case – though there surely was in the former. It was anticipated in the tale "The Poet" in *Seven Gothic Tales*. The danger is that of applying the pattern of the puppet show and the story – this tale betokens the transition between the two – to the life of flesh and warm blood. This story is a protest against that idea and expresses a deep irony occasioned by it. The figure of the counsellor in it might feel he is in the hands of Shakespeare and Goethe. But the lovers, Anders and Fransine, have not felt or wanted to feel themselves in the hands of any author. However, the dying counsellor confuses his own plot with the great poets' plays. "My poor girl," he says, "Everything is good." And he tells her that they are all "sacred puppets". He speaks generally and does not say in whose hands they are. However, Fransine makes no mistake. Now, at this unbearable moment, she realises that she and Anders have been in the hands of the counsellor and cries as she kills him: "You! You poet!" When this story is considered in relation to "The Cardinal's First Tale", the question naturally arises as to whether Isak Dinesen has repressed the theme, worked it out at a deeper level or simply given it a more stringent interpretation. Or perhaps it could be said that she began with a caricature of the theme – the failure – and finished with the positive version – its success.

NO IDENTITY AT ALL

Between these two extreme ways of discovering and realising one's identity there is a third possibility: not to have an identity at all, and not to suffer from this lack, but consciously and resolutely to escape identity, and to experience this state as a relief, a permanent adventure and pleasure. This bold, indecisive condition is revealed in the theme of "The Dreamers" from *Seven Gothic Tales*.

The principal character in the tale is Pellegrina, a superb singer at the Milan Opera, beloved and fêted by everyone, the rich, the noble and the poor. She is badly hurt in a fire in the theatre, and as a result of her injuries and the shock she loses her voice, never to sing again. She recovers physically, but in her deep despair she considers taking her own life because without her voice she feels like the living dead. Dead, because she *was* her voice, her voice was her identity. She tries to bring herself to commit suicide, but in the end she refrains and resolves to live on. This decision is the crucial point in the tale, the reason for the chain of events that constitutes it, and the starting point for it, though the account of the accident and of Pellegrina's decision is delayed until the end.

Pellegrina has a very special friend, a rich old Jew called Marcus Cocoza. From the first moment he heard her sing he has worshipped her, felt her to be a bringer of joy, and understood, as he says, "the meaning of heaven and earth, of the stars, life and death, and eternity." He has become her friend and bought her a villa near Milan. Because of her generous radiant expectations, which have met but scant response, she has always been deeply disappointed in love and has been somewhat ashamed of herself. When her affairs have finished she has turned to her friend and helper, and they have had their platonic pleasures and the sublime joy of being together. And thus they have lived in the white villa at Milan until the day of her disaster. During her illness and convalescence she is tormented by despair and the feeling that all joy and meaning in life have been irretrievably lost. In spite of this she gives up her intention of committing suicide; a spark is struck in the darkness, and an idea for a possible way out begins to develop within her. She is dead to the splendid life she has known – but feels reborn to another. This new life is not a pale imitation of what she has lost, no compensation for it, but something quite different, something radically new and never before heard of. One day, early in the morning, before sunrise, she sends for her friend, and in the pergola outside the house she tells him of her thoughts:

"This disaster of mine, had it happened to someone else – say now, Marcus, to a soprano of China, of the Imperial Opera of China, a hundred years ago – we might have heard of it, and not have thought much about it, or wept many tears over it. Still, it would have been as sad and as terrible. But because it happened to Pellegrina, it seemed to us too cruel to bear. This, my Marcus, it need not be, and it shall not be so for us again."

Now she explains to him how she will live her future life. He shall help her to tell the world that Pellegrina is dead, make a grave for her, and erect a monument on it. "Nobody," she says, "must ever be Pellegrina again. To have her once more upon the stage of life, of this hard world, and to have such awful things happen to her as do happen to people on the earth – no, that must not be thought of. No human being could stand the thought." He promises to do as she wishes. Below them, on the road, they now see some men and women going out to work in the fields. She points to a couple of the women and tries to imagine their state of mind: perhaps one is happy for some reason, and another unhappy for some other reason. "What do we think of that, Marcus, you and I?" she asks, and concludes: Not much. Thereupon she comes to the essence of her new insight and explains her intention:

"I will be that now. The time has come for me to be that: a woman called one name or another. And if she is unhappy we shall not think a great deal about it."

"And if I come to think very much of what happens to that one woman, why, I shall go away at once, and be someone else: a woman who makes lace in the town, or who teaches children to read, or a lady travelling to Jerusalem to pray at the Holy Sepulchre. There are many that I can be. If they are happy or unhappy, or if they are fools or wise people, those women, I shall not think a great deal about that. Neither will you, if you hear about it. I will not be one person again, Marcus, I will be always many persons from now. Never again will I have my heart and my whole life bound up with one woman, to suffer so much. It is terrible to me to think of it even. That, you see, I have done long enough. I cannot be asked to do it any more. It is all over."

"And you, Marcus, you have given me many things; now I shall give you this good advice. Be many people. Give up this game of being one and of being always Marcus Cocoza, so that you have been really his slave and his prisoner. You have not done anything without first considering how it would affect Marcus Coco-za's prestige. You must, from now, be more than one, many people, as many as you can think of. I feel, Marcus – that all people in the world ought to be, each of them, more than one, and they would all, yes, all of them, be more easy at heart. They would have a little fun. Is it not strange, that no philosopher has thought of this, and that I should hit upon it?"

At last she says that she and Marcus must part. He then proposes that he should follow her and be near her, so that she can send for him if she needs a friend to help her. She consents:

"Yes, do that. Be near me, Marcus, so that if ever anyone should mistake me for Pellegrina Leoni, I can get hold of you, and you can help me to get away. – But speak to me you must never. I could not hear your voice without remembering the divine voice of Pellegrina, and her great triumphs, and this house – and the garden."

Then they part, and her new life begins with its different roles and love affairs, pleasures and risks. After the main plot there are, as it were, three sub-plots. In three different disguises and situations she meets three men: as a prostitute in Rome, as a milliner and revolutionary in Lucerne, and as a saintly principal of a village school and hospital. The three young men are fascina-ted by her and involved as in a matter of life and death, but in every case, when it comes to a decision, Pellegrina disappears without trace. In his own individual way each of the three fails to recover from the impression she has made on him and the great expectations she has evoked, and they all seek for her every-where. Accidentally, or guided by destiny, or at the behest of the divine author, the three meet in a hotel in the mountains near a pass between Switzerland and Italy. They sit talking and drink-ing wine, and two of them tell of a remarkable woman they have met – Pellegrina in one of her disguises. From time to time new guests arrive, and suddenly a lady and her maid pass through the room. "That was she," says one of the young men. But when asked about her the porter replies that none of the names they propose is that of the lady, adding that she has hired a carriage and has left. Now the three hire another carriage and pursue her. The weather is terrible. They are overcome by a snowstorm. The carriage sticks in a snowdrift, and they continue on foot to discover that her vehicle, too, has come to a halt, and that she has left it. At last they catch up with her and demand to know who she is. She claims not to recognise the three questioners. Confronted with three mirror images of three different women, three different images of her temporary identities in their minds, she becomes desperate. Every time she has been with one of them in the past, she has escaped at the critical moment and changed her identity. But now she is cornered. The three have seen a snakelike scar on her neck, a result of the fire at the theatre. Now they determine to identify her, using force if necessary. At this moment she runs across the road and flings herself into the abyss. She lies seemingly dead on a ledge, and with great difficulty they manage to drag her up; the old Jew has by now arrived in his coach and she is taken in it to the hotel. While she lies on a stretcher in a large room and they all keep watch beside her, the old Jew tells her story. He reveals not who she is, but who she was.

In sketching "The Dreamers" I have begun from the inside, from the core. In reality the story is told as an enigma within an enigma within an enigma. When it is compared with "The Cardinal's First Tale", it emerges that the woman, who is no longer Pellegrina, does not derive her temporary identities from the stories in which she is involved, but from the new roles which she has assumed, indeed created. Yet *Pellegrina* had an identity. Where did she derive it from? She herself proclaims the answer when she asks Marcus, her friend and helper, to put upon the marble slab on her grave, in addition to her name and the dates of her birth and death, the inscription: *By the grace of God.* With the perfection and magnificence of her voice, of her song, she has fulfilled God's plan for her. There can be no doubt about it: "The Dreamers" is much closer to the major themes in "Peter and Rosa" and the African memoirs than to "The Cardinal's First

Tale", as is also borne out by the references in it to wild animals.

To begin with there is her name: Pellegrina Leoni – a subtle combination of falcon and lion. The lady in black, the Cardinal's penitent, is not compared to a single animal. How different is the case of Pellegrina: She is like a young shark in the sea, like a winged lioness, like a python, like an albatross, graceful like the wise and gentle gazelles, on her last flight like an angry owl on a branch, or like a crane when it runs along the ground to catch the wind. She is likened to a falcon, wild and mad with fear, and at last, when she leaps into the abyss, to a black martin as it launches itself from a slope or a roof to take flight. And on her deathbed, when she awakens and thinks she is Pellegrina resurrected, ready to sing in *Don Giovanni*, there comes no song from her, but only what is described as "a strange sound, like the distant roar of a great animal".

That all these comparisons are not arbitrary poetical devices or mere images, but are intended to take the theme to its furthest consequence, is confirmed at the end of the story. There, Isak Dinesen lets Lincoln, the narrator and one of Pellegrina's lovers, say, as he imagines what would have happened to Pellegrina if she had not died that night:

"In the end, I have thought, she might perhaps have decided to become a pretty little jackal, and have made herself a den on the plain, or upon the slope of a hill. I have imagined that so vividly that on a moonlit night I have believed that I heard her voice amongst the hills. And I have seen her, then, running about, playing with her own small graceful shadow, having a little ease of heart, a little fun."

ULTIMATE IDENTITY

Finally, how did these different concepts of identity work out in Isak Dinesen's own life? In the course of a discussion about "The Dreamers" I once said to her: "You are Pellegrina". She answered: "Yes, I am," adding: "The loss of her voice corresponds to my loss of the farm and Africa." Next she expounded on how it came to mean that she had lost her destiny and her identity, and that from that time on she had *willed* not to have a destiny, *willed* not to suffer under any identity. In turn I told her of the tremendous impact the tale had made on me when I read it for the first time at the age of twenty. She replied that this story was so powerful precisely because it was the first she had written after she lost the farm and returned to Denmark. "It is like a scream, a lion's roar," she said. "I could not write *Out of Africa* until the pain abated."

As a storyteller Isak Dinesen had, of course, her private life. To me, before I met her, she was only the famous writer, indeed, so impersonal and famous that I thought her dead. However, during the time I knew her it became clear to me how many roles she played and how differently she behaved towards different people. I often wondered at this at the time, but subsequently I have realised that it was a major reason why people formed such vastly different impressions and opinions of her, and why they could bitterly disagree as to what kind of person she was. Of course, her role playing did not go to such extremes as with Pellegrina, and it lasted only for some hours, a day or an evening at a time. The very use of pseudonyms, after her time in Africa, is part of her role playing.

If, at the end of her life, she had one recurring role, it was that of being a storyteller, like Mira in "The Dreamers", almost anonymous, forgetting her past in the indulgent passion for telling a story. Keats, in advance of his time as a poet, and still more advanced in his reflections on poetry, wrote in a letter from 1818, three years before he died: "The Sun, – the Moon, – the Sea – and men and women, who are creatures of impulse, are poetical, and have about them an unchangeable attribute; the poet has none, no identity –." In the light of all this it becomes apparent that Isak Dinesen as a writer was made up of a mixture of extremely modern and extremely archaic elements. But, in contrast to Keats and Mira, she suffered at times from a terrible hubris. In the beginning was the story; such is the Cardinal's thesis – and hers. But who makes the story? Not God, but a human being, once anonymous, forgotten like the builders of the pyramids and the first cathedrals, but now whether or not his or her work is appreciated, a real person whose name is known. Now, as a maker of stories she was tempted to apply this fundamental ability of hers to make a story of life, involving living persons attracted by the magnetic field of her personality. She foresaw the risk, as is indicated in "The Poet" from *Seven Gothic Tales*, but as indicated above, she toughened and repeated the pattern. I, at least, have had it applied to myself. And certainly there is a great and moving irony in the fact that so many of her tales deal with persons who violate the essence and plan of the story in which they are involved.

However, there was one thing in her life which I am sure was not a role: her concern for, and loyalty to, her real friends and the squatters on the farm. And, throughout her life, her concern and fondness for the animals. Her constant and close relationship to them, especially the wild animals, was not only an act of identification in order to achieve identity, betokened during her time in Africa by her determination to protect them and their habitat. In *Out of Africa* she has movingly pictured the sad fate of the wild animals in the zoos of Europe and expressed her intense loathing of this degradation to which they are subjected. At the end of her life she was tireless in her efforts to defend animals against the torture of vivisection. With this end in view she embarked on profound and subtle lectures and articles, which involved her in painful and depressing discussions with scientists defending as necessary the use of experimental animals and reducing her profound understanding of and insight into the being and essence of animals to sentimental ignorance. She also made a direct attempt to influence the legislators who in 1952 were to revise the law protecting animals. She organised and collected signatures for a petition seeking once and for all the prohibition of experiments with dogs because of their close friendship with man. She failed – but did succeed in one last action before she died: in turning the park of Rungstedlund into a bird sanctuary.

There is in our civilisation a deeply-rooted suspicion of people who admire and love animals and believe they have rights; this attitude is seen as something exotic and strange, or anthropomorphic and sentimental, or as a kind of spiritual sodomy. People of that observance cannot expect to be taken quite seriously, at least not in that respect. It was quite obvious that the scientists with whom Isak Dinesen discussed her views were confused. How could a world-famous author speak as though animals had any rights, when human beings thanks to experiments with animals could be cured of all manner of serious illnesses? What she had written about animals in her works might well be admirable as mere poetry, fairytales and fantasies, but how could such fantasies be employed as arguments to defend animals in real life, in our times.

Yet it is impossible to ignore this dimension of Isak Dinesen's character and personality and still seemingly to take her seriously. For here she is not acting a part, but feels herself to be fulfilling an essential part of God's plan for her. And I am convinced that it is no mere coincidence when, in "The Cardinal's First Tale", devoid of animals and centred on the story itself, she refers to Saint Thomas Aquinas, to whom animals only existed for the sake of man, to be used by man – while in her African memoirs, absorbed in her admiration and love for the wild animals and identifying with them, she refers to Saint Francis of Assisi, embracing them and including them in his "Canticle to the Sun". And the second last remark of Miss Malin in "The Deluge at Norderney", unexpected and seemingly without any reference to the final lines, is like a distant echo expressing the feelings of the young Calypso and the spirit of Saint Francis:

"I, too, was once a young girl. I walked in the woods and looked at the birds, and I thought: How dreadful that people shut up birds in cages. I thought: If I could so live and so serve the world that after me there should never again be birds in cages, they should all be free –."

Thorkild Bjørnvig

44

ISAK DINESEN/ KAREN BLIXEN

The Empty Space
Between Art and Church

by *Aage Henriksen*

If it is true, as so many women claim today, that women make up not only half of the population, but also half of the meanings of life, then it is true today only because it has always been so. But then the assertion opens up the prospect of historical critique and elucidation which have to do not only with various forms of cohabitation but with morality and theology as well.

When Karen Blixen as one of her standard paradoxes professed that she was 3000 years old, then probably it is a linguistic short form which was meant to indicate the historical span of her consciousness of the constant but often unseen presence of the feminine. The formula for this presence, she herself has outlined in *Daguerreotypes:* "It is the secret power of the feminine: the intimated." The meaning of this sentence is not that women distinguish themselves by special intuitions but that they arouse notions in the male consciousness with their faces and bodies and – when they become aware of this – by signs and words and actions. Thereby they participate, even when they seem not to participate, and when they do not control the steps of men, they control their thoughts. Thus the erotic sphere has a far wider extension than one would ordinarily assume, and it turns out to be a consciousness-shaping force. I am quite aware that this is not satisfactory as a feminist basis today, where everything is a question of social visibility, but this point of view opens up the prospect for other perspectives that would have otherwise been closed. As a matter of fact, this rests on our childhood knowledge, that a human being is a man and a woman, as it says in *Genesis,* and this admits us to areas where we thought mankind was not allowed.

With these introductory remarks I have opened up a vast and airy space. I shall now attempt to build a staircase ascending it.

In one of her shortest tales, "The Ring", Karen Blixen has delineated the prototype which is the basis of all her stories. It concerns a young 19-year-old girl. A week ago she was married to the young squire of whom she has been fond since they played together as children. They have had some trouble marrying each other, but now things are settled and she enthusiastically takes command over her little kingdom. It is – quite as she has been told that reality is – a small orderly and decent place which is suspended in a larger, overall lawfulness and decency. She has found her place. Her dreams of reality coincide with what she sees around her – and she imagines an endless line of carefree, happy days. Now she can fully expose her inner being and nothing hidden or secret can come between her husband and herself. But a week after her wedding in a clearing in the wood, she is accidentally confronted with a hunted outlaw, a boy her own age. His face is bruised and smashed, his hands are dark and soiled, and his clothes torn to shreds. This sight upsets her and she is frightened, not of what he might do to her, but by the fact that he exists, for he is incompatible with her idea of reality. But within the few moments they face each other, he begins to exist for her. At the moment when he attempts to, as it were, extinguish himself by closing his eyes and setting her free, he becomes real for her. And when she is back in the open park once more, safe and unharmed, she feels that she has devoted herself to something. "To what? To poverty, outlawry, total desolation. To the sin and sorrow of the entire world." Concealing her newfound insight she rejoins her husband – with the insurmountable secret like a wall between them.

In miniature, this recognition is the underlying principle of all of Karen Blixen's works. Parallels can be drawn to The Book of Job, the biblical text which Blixen quotes most often and most convincingly. Honest to the core Job too, as you know, falls silent when he sees his orderly and simple reality transformed into a dream, which is let into a larger, more dangerous, unpredictable reality which includes everything that criminally and sacredly lies outside the law.

The process of thought which is indicated here is not, of course, entirely surprising. It has been at work in the European consciousness during the last 150 years. For Marx and Freud and the natural sciences, visible everyday life, regulated by good sense and morality, is merely a reflection of impersonal forces which never even reach the consciousness of those who act in an everyday world. Unlike these predominant modes of thought, however, Karen Blixen does not arrive at her ideas of the subconscious via theoretical constructions or laboratory experiments. Like so many of the great women writers of our time, among them Iris Murdoch and Doris Lessing, Blixen is at one and the same time a storyteller and a thinker. This double focus of the consciousness means that she always has to start within the everyday lives of the people who wish, act, and speak. Her subject could, with Goethe's expression be called "the apparent secrets," the secrets that are just in front of one's eyes, but which only a few experience and reflect on. In that way with her completely attentive observation and empathetic imagination for consequences, slowly she created a universe for herself, which simultaneously was modern, highly original, and ancient.

There is not much doubt of how she first arrived at these ideas. The shape in which she first encountered the subconscious and the invisible, was the traditionally religious one. As is well known, she grew up in an environment where discourse was governed by a strictly moralistic Christianity. This became an indelible part of her own consciousness as well, although she turned against it in opposition. What she heard did not correspond with what she saw. Out of this conflict grew a desire to recapture the visible, sensual, natural world and to pursue the natural passions to their farthest, most hidden recesses.

Several years after she had made her first decisions in this matter, she displayed them as part of a speech she gave for Ole Wivel on her 65th birthday. The most obvious occasion was that Ole Wivel and Martin A. Hansen as the new editors of the literary periodical *Heretica* had announced a new direction which would merge art with moral responsibility. This brought her to speak on the ambiguous and sensuous nature of art which undermines any moralization and about the conflict between a religious and a heroic-atheistic view of life which she knew from childhood and which – in Africa – was a perfectly resolved and reconciled conflict. Heavenly love and earthly love were not regarded as contradictions out there as they are with the Christian Europeans, as apparently they were in Martin A. Hansen and now in *Heretica;* a contagion from the dualistic tradition itself. "I am warning you," she continued, "against your moral choice and inclinations towards the ethical. Has not this exact choice in our protestant cultures led us, against our very own intentions, straight into the abyss? Has not Christianity excluded the enthusiasm over the gifts and mysteries of this life, renounced and repressed our sensuality? And thereby blocked us out of the spiritual world on the only conditions that we have." Later in her speech, she mentioned that in her youth she had heard two of the outstanding personalities of the Danish folk high school movement, Holger Begtrup and Jakob Knudsen give public speeches and had felt repelled. Only later did she realize that the reason for her reaction was that these two men, who were powerful and articulate, and more than slightly conceited, spoke against their own charisma – about the fragility and impotence of the human race.

Her observation is of the kind that we know so well from many literary works, which austerely reveal how the things men say and imagine are meant merely to obscure the much feebler things they do and are. But Karen Blixen makes a different use of the well-known instrument than the conventional. She uses it, not as a moral tool for castigation, but on the contrary, to show how the natural passions deeply pervade the official virtue and unencumberedly reach their goals precisely because of the slack and vague character of virtue and piety.

This attitude, now, has two far-reaching consequences, both of which are surprising, and while I develop the first, the second cannot be inferred. The first is that a certain pattern, one could call it a genre within the narrative genre, is repeated in Blixen's works. A ceremony takes place. It is conducted like a familiar Christian feast or festival, the Sacrament or celebration of Pentecost, but if one takes a closer look, it turns out that what is really conducted under this pious cover is a pagan mystery. The major example of this is "The Deluge at Norderney", in a more compact form it is repeated in "Heloise", "Babette's Feast", and "The Last Day". I shall have to limit myself to discussing the shorter texts.

The stories are based on the undeniably well-known fact about human love relationships, that they are complicated. As in the animal world, one sex is attracted to the other, but if that were the whole matter, then already at this point love would be as uncomplicated as Lenin assumed it would be after the revolution: "As simple as drinking a glass of water." But, as we all know, this general instinct is most powerfully unleashed in the meeting of two individuals. *People* fall in love. Their individuality, their social identities are pervaded by the nature of their instincts, and from this circumstance emanate all the well-known deformations, illusions, and breakthroughs to surprising discoveries that love is probably not what at first we thought it was.

The horizontal solution to the problems of love is so familiar, so excellent that it is unnecessary for me to mention or recommend it. On the other solution, however, I shall have to dwell for a few moments. We could call it the vertical solution, because up and down pervade each other, the instinctual impulses rise and pour themselves into consciousness and self-consciousness.

What we are talking about here, of course, is the individualization of the impulses. You could argue that all magic tricks and artifices on erotic grounds, in fiction, in psychoanalysis and in day to day reality, consist of interfering with and fracturing the psychosomatic system, in which the anonymous and the individual desires are united. An object picture might be useful here. In Jakob Burchardt's *The Renaissance in Italy*, is printed a reproduction of a picture by the painter Angelo Bronzino, entitled *Lucrezia*. It portrays a beautiful woman who is staring searchingly, straight out of the picture at the spectator. Her right breast is exposed and swelling out at the observer, who might feel attracted were it not for the fact that in her left hand, extended upwards, she is holding a long pointed knife, which one must assume to be as sharp as it is pointed.

Simultaneously she urges, allures and repels, but what in this manner is elicited and incapable of reaching its object, subsequently goes its own inner ways. This Lucrezia with her ambiguous appearance calls to mind the biblical Judith, whose story is told in one of the Apocrypha. When I mention her here it is because soon we shall reencounter her. She defeats Holofernes, Israel's enemy, by means of her beauty alone:

"She anointed her face with ointment and fastened her hair with a tiara and put on a linen gown to deceive him. Her sandal ravished his eyes, her beauty captivated his mind, and the sword severed his neck."

This might be the right time to remind you that this ambiguity of the erotic, which I have suggested, has played a crucial part up through European history in Christian sects and lodges. There an attempt was made to separate what is naturally united. On the one hand an ascending spiritual development was encouraged with several means, but at the same time – in the midst of societies that were narrowminded and terrified of sex – an attempt was made to develop a liberated but controlled sensuality. The latter not simply in an attempt to create an increased *joie de vivre*, but also to tie up sensuality to worldly conditions, the only place where sensuality is requited. The purpose of this was to prevent sensuality from serpentinely following the spiritual stream inwards and upwards. In Mozart's *The Magic Flute*, this division is performed and the double wedding illustrated in a famous and festive line of images.

But in Karen Blixen's tales, it is the opposite strategy, that of merging, which governs their progress.

Most admirably and with the complete enthusiastic endorsement of the reader, this happens in the tale "Heloise". It is set during the Franco-Prussian war in 1870, and concerns a French company of travellers who are stranded in an inn behind German lines. Their lives now depend on the young German officer who is in command there. It now turns out, to his horror and enthralment, that the person he is to negotiate with is the dazzling French beauty, Heloise. A power struggle takes place between them, which evolves so that the desires she arouses with her splendour, she expels by means of unlimited impertinence and scorn. This does not exterminate his desires, which instead travel other, invisible roads within him. And it is then characteristic of Heloise as of Blixen's other female characters and indeed of Karen Blixen herself, that, despite everything, she is capable of meeting and capturing the desires which stream towards goals that are hidden to the world, so that later she can praise their strength.

A little while ago I said that the reader enthusiastically is on Heloise's side and stands behind her, but maybe, after all, the reader of this story, whether male or female, gets a little ill at ease when the back cloths of the story are pulled up one by one. Closest behind the story one finds Maupassant's tale "Boule de suif", on which "Heloise" clearly is parallelled. It takes place in exactly the same setting but concerns the humiliations of a woman. Behind this story emerges Rousseau's *La nouvelle Héloïse*, and behind this story about psychological destruction of love emerges the medieval romance of Heloise and Abailard and his mutilation. All the way at the back lies the myth of Venus and Adonis. And on all these back cloths, what we call love has left its traces of humiliation and violence, castration and death.

More peculiar than the Heloise figure and surrounded with a sweeter and more beautiful magic, is the 15-year-old girl in the tale "The Last Day". This story takes place on Whitsunday of 1852, and the opening of the tale is preoccupied with considerations over where and in what shape the Holy Spirit would emerge if on its feast-day it visited Copenhagen. It does not arrive, instead Odin appears, but in the shape of one of his most alluring valkyries. *She* is described thus by the young man who first sets eyes on her in a clearing in the woods, where she emerges in a gleam:

"She was so exquisite that she beamed. She looked straight at me with her eyes wide open, like the bright eyes of a hawk, and her gaze was not mild, no, it was stern, wild, one might think that she was angry with one. But at the same time it was infinitely friendly and encouraging. She knew everything and laughed at the danger."

But I must limit myself to discussing the central scene of this complicated story, which illuminates all the others. As the adopted daughter of a minister, the above-mentioned young girl takes care of an old sailor in the parish, the uncle Valdemar of the narrator. In his prime, uncle Valdemar was a great womanizer and has many proud conquests behind him. But now, for several years, he has been sitting in his chair, paralyzed from the waist down, feeling that neither life nor death want anything to do with him. He fears dying in the straw – just like the mythical Nordic warriors, because this would lead them down to Hel. But uncle Valdemar's discouragement during his long and weary process of disintegration changes to hope when the minister's daughter starts to visit him. And all his hopes are redeemed on his last day which passes thus: The girl sits and reads to him from the Bible, from the last chapter of The Book of Judith, Judith's triumphal song. The old man persuades her to move closer to him, and finally he rises up by clinging to her. Also his manhood rises one last time. He kisses her while she holds on to his long white hair and his face starts to glow. "But the next moment she pushed him away with a swift, frantic movement, and thereby he tumbled down sidelong to her feet." There on the floor, now, lies uncle Valdemar with a solemn, triumphant, glowing face. And dies. And the young girl has the same serious, triumphantly glowing face.

She *does* break his neck, there is no denying that. But she does it out of sheer kindness, in quiet empathy, of pure technical necessity – so as to prevent the stream which has finally reached the halls of Valhalla in his skull, from being sucked down again.

Excepting the final acts of Goethe's *Faust* and *The Tibetan Book of the Dead*, nowhere in literature have I encountered such intimacy with death and the arterial roads through which the soul can move.

When Karen Blixen conceived of her plan of turning against Christian morality and duality to follow the natural passions into their inner recesses instead, she was enabled to uncover experiences as ancient and forgotten as the Dead Sea Scrolls. This was the first consequence of the plan. The reader who adjusts himself to see her perspective and is perhaps even radiated by her perspicacity may identify with the young wife in "The Ring": "The world is different, unfamiliar, yet recognizable; I have to reconsider all things." Thereby we are led into the other surprising consequence of the original plan. It has to do with the costs and once again poses the problem of dualism.

What Blixen said about dualism to Ole Wivel, she once wrote to me: "You say that nature has no memory, but I have often wished that I had the memory of a tree, which carries each and every single annual ring stamped into its being. I am altogether incapable of comprehending a 'dualism'." And it *is* true: the universe of her tales is natural, erotic, and no ways out of it are indicated. But it is not so hermetic that there are not ways in – from an unknown, undescribed space of possibilities. The men who force their way into full visible identity in her tales pay for their victory with their lives. What kind of lives? The deaths they experience could be described as murders, as when the butler Kaspersen kills his master, the cardinal. More often, however, these deaths are suggested merely as an imperceptible dwindling of longing, a discontinuation of the ability to love. A source of light withdraws from their lives to return to its own space.

The uneasiness which arises for the reader from these vague but perpetually repeated clues, indeed harmonizes perfectly with the fact that Karen Blixen did not present herself as a person who was liberated on all sides in the terms of modern science. Quite the reverse: when I met her, and when other people met her, she said that she had died many years ago, and in the most hair-raising fashion and to the confusion and despair of her friends, she defined herself within the Christian tradition as a witch, and a serpent, and the friend of the Devil. This was not a whim, not a joke once uttered, but something which she claimed as her right, the essential note on all texts. But thus, of course, dualism re-emerges in a new shape as a relationship between the life which is included in her works and that which is excluded. The tremendous expansion contains its own disintegration.

The best answer to this enigma is probably another question: Why do we, who were young 30 years ago, need precisely her and not more Godfearing individuals? Why do so many people need her today? To this question she once gave me an answer which applies to others beside myself. She said: "As long as I live it will be bothersome for you to have to deal with me. But when I am dead, what happened to me when my mother died and I kept vigil over her at night, will happen to you. Then I saw not just the old woman, but also the young wife, and the happy little girl. And then I understood many things I had not understood before."

This advice builds a bridge over the terrifying ambiguity in Karen Blixen's being and works, and if followed, it can lead one beyond the limits of the universe which she controlled so powerfully. Only then does what she said of herself turn out to be true: "I am a messenger who has been sent on a long journey to declare that there is hope in the world."

Aage Henriksen

Translated by Annette Wernblad

Selected Works by ISAK DINESEN/KAREN BLIXEN:

Syv fantastiske fortællinger. [Seven Gothic Tales]. [Short stories]. Copenhagen: Reitzel, 1935.*

Den afrikanske farm. [Out of Africa]. [Memoirs]. Copenhagen: Gyldendal, 1937.*

Vinter eventyr. [Winter's Tales]. [Stories]. Copenhagen: Gyldendal, 1942.*

Gengældelsens veje. [The Angelic Avengers]. [Novel written under pseudonym Pierre Andrézel]. Tr. into Danish by Clara Svendsen. Copenhagen: Gyldendal, 1944.*

Daguerreotypier. [Daguerreotypes and Other Essays]. [Essays]. Copenhagen: Gyldendal, 1951.*

Sidste fortællinger. [Last Tales]. [Stories]. Copenhagen: Gyldendal, 1957.*

Skæbne anekdoter. [Anecdotes of Destiny]. [Stories]. Copenhagen: Gyldendal, 1958.*

Skygger på græsset. [Shadows on the Grass]. [Memoirs]. Copenhagen: Gyldendal, 1960.*

Ehrengard. [Ehrengard]. [Short story]. Tr. into Danish by Clara Svendsen. Copenhagen: Gyldendal, 1963.*

Efterladte fortællinger. [Posthumous Tales]. Ed. by Frans Lasson. [Short stories]. Copenhagen: Gyldendal, 1975.*

Breve fra Afrika: 1914-1931. [Letters from Africa: 1914-1931]. Ed. by Frans Lasson. Copenhagen: Gyldendal, 1978.*

*Published in English:

Seven Gothic Tales. New York: Harrison Smith and Robert Hass, 1934. London: Putnam, 1934.

Out of Africa. London: Putnam, 1937. New York: Random House, 1938.

Winter's Tales. New York: Random House; London: Putnam, 1942.

Last Tales. New York: Random House; London: Putnam: 1957.

Anecdotes of Destiny. New York: Random House; London: Michael Joseph, 1958.

Shadows on the Grass. New York: Random House; London: Michael Joseph, 1961.

Ehrengard. New York: Random House; London: Michael Joseph, 1963.

The Angelic Avengers. Chicago and London: University of Chicago Press, 1975.

Carnival: Entertainments and Posthumous Tales. Chicago: University of Chicago Press, 1977.

Daguerreotypes and Other Essays. Tr. by P. M. Mitchell and W. D. Paden. Chicago: University of Chicago Press, 1979.

Letters from Africa: 1914-1931. Ed. by Frans Lasson. Tr. by Anne Born. Chicago: University of Chicago Press, 1981.

Works about ISAK DINESEN/KAREN BLIXEN in English:

Henriksen, Liselotte. *Isak Dinesen: A Bibliography.* [Complete, annotated bibliography of works by and about Isak Dinesen]. Copenhagen: Gyldendal, 1977.

Juhl, Marianne and Jørgensen, Bo Hakon. *Diana's Revenge.* Odense: University of Odense, 1985.

Thurman, Judith. *Isak Dinesen: The Life of Karen Blixen.* London: Weidenfeld & Nicolson, 1982.

For further reference see: *A Bibliography of Danish Literature in English Translation 1950-1980.* Copenhagen: Det danske Selskab, 1982.

KIRSTEN THORUP

It's Thorup Today

by *Torben Brostrøm*

Kirsten Thorup's third book, published in 1969, is called *Love from Trieste*. The title is taken from the greeting on the postcard that introduces this collection of texts which might perhaps be called poems, perhaps fragments of a novel. The postcard has been sent by a certain John, though to whom we are not told. It tells, in brief, of resentment, of disappointment with emotional involvement. John is, it says, tempted to be content with a life on the surface. Trieste triste.

Through the many short, laconic texts the reader senses an emotional triangle, the relationship between the girl friends Maja and Q, and then John. He gradually supplants Maja. The last text but one bears the title "Farewell to the last really warm day". It runs thus: "Against her will she blushed when she discovered that the nylon stockings she had just bought and was now holding in her hand had the same name as her lover." This juxtaposition of the object of her affections and something for everyday use is again indicative of superficiality and the reification of feelings, but also of impulses that are no more than noted. They are not treated in depth, but they represent part of the atmosphere surrounding the characters, as is emphasised by the very last words in the book, which the reader is presumably intended to ascribe to Q: "Call me eau-de-cologne".

Kafka portrayed his K wandering around in the anonymous city with his trial taking place both inside and outside himself, committed only to his own superficiality. In his novels Kierkegaard let the intellectual aesthetes analyse their own lack of passion as they followed their seductive pursuits in Copenhagen. Hamsun had his starving hero misunderstand the beautiful Ylajali in the streets of Christiania. But what of Thorup and Trieste?

Italo Svevo's novel *Senilitá* from 1898 was published in Danish in 1964 (English translation *As a Man Grows Old*, 1962). It concerns the half-hearted love of a civil servant Emilio for Angiolina: "They always met outdoors. They went walking out together in the streets of Trieste's suburbs. After their early meetings they gave up Sant' Andrea, where there were too many people, and for a time Via Opicina with its two rows of chestnut trees became their preferred meeting place."

This passage is used as a quotation in *Love from Trieste*, thus linking it to Svevo. Otherwise there is no local colour, the milieu is generalised and international. In an interview Kirsten Thorup has said that she has never been to Trieste. Aesthetically speaking, the town's role is to indicate the homelessness of the characters, to show them as divided between consciousness and background. The reference to Svevo and thereby to the other European writers concerned with the big city, points to a thematic affinity representing what in general terms can be called disharmony. Doubt as to one's own identity and the permanence of feeling. The schizophrenia of everyday life. The divided self.

Meanwhile, Kirsten Thorup's novel from Trieste is not a novel, but a selection of fragments which dispel any sense of plot or of causally determined actions. The book's field of consciousness is based on a number of impulses. One section is called "Maja's Memoirs", but her memory overall is broken down into a number of brief momentary reminiscences. And it is not entirely certain that they all derive from the same memory. The quotation from Svevo refers to John and Q, but now Maja recalls how she herself used to wander around in the suburban streets arm in arm with John, eating sweets – just like Emilio and Angiolina.

This is the realm of speculative feeling. "I tried to feel as I was standing in front of the mirror," observes Maja. But, as her name presumably indicates, she only sees through a veil.

There is an exotic air about Kirsten Thorup's little book. This results not from the milieu, but from the backcloth of feelings glimpsed, from the soft velvet of despair, from the sweetness of indifference, from the seductive power of emptiness and momentary void. Eau de Cologne. It was not written by Kierkegaard or Hamsun, Svevo or Kafka. It was devised and composed by a woman.

It could even be seen as a reply to Svevo's *Senilitá*, which is distinguished by its detailed analysis and its treatment of shades of feeling, the constant watch kept on the author's own reactions and those of others. This is the Kierkegaardian, male, tradition. Throughout all Kirsten Thorup's work we have a suspicion which is not always easy to explain that her characters are not expressing themselves, that they are also someone else, perhaps in reality someone completely different, a third person even.

She started writing in the 1960s, before the women's movement really got going, before the new self-assuredness of feminism developed. There were signs of it, and it was typically expressed in the form of momentary awareness in the works of her contemporaries. The same year as *Love from Trieste* saw Charlotte Strandgaard's novel *They Love Each Other at Times*, a love story in 81 short notes. The following year came Dorrit Willumsen's *tea spice acrylic fee grasshopper* (1970), a novel even the title of which points to human alienation and discontinuity. And at the same time Inger Christensen wrote *It*, her lyrical story of creation leading up to the disharmony brought about by dread.

This was the time when anti-psychiatry was being discussed, and when R. D. Laing's books hit the market and attracted fresh attention to schizophrenia as a mental and social reaction pattern. Literature of the time produced enormous amounts of material to document the human experience of being at once *inside and outside*. This is the title of Thorup's first volume of poems from 1967. Here we meet vaguely characterised people in indeterminate places, parties and gatherings with which we feel no sense of familiarity. There is all the time *something else*. It can be sensed either as an undiscovered quality or as a new void. A potential for madness.

In this first book, the 25-year-old Kirsten Thorup wrote her way into a modernist tradition which was not new in itself, but which now acquired a new accent. She herself had experienced enough changes of surroundings to acquire the modern experiences of rootlessness, inability to make contact, and impersonality, which lead into that abstract life that knows no growth or development but which fragments existence into overwhelming, uninterpretable flashes of reality. This is the stuff poetry is made of, or that special, abruptly realistic prose towards which Kirsten Thorup was groping her way. She was born in 1942 in the small town of Gelsted on the island of Funen, where her father was a newsagent and bookseller. One could, however, scarcely talk of a book-loving family background, and indeed on the contrary, Kirsten Thorup's high school career betokened a breach with the family tradition. Her familiarity with social outcasts stems partly from her contact with boys from a nearby community home, a job in the mental hospital in Middelfart and a period living in the very mixed district of Vesterbro in Copenhagen. Teeming impressions of people and their usual unusual qualities. Material taken from everyday life is obviously absorbed into the visions of the world as seen in her writing.

Outside yourself
you dissolve
into mycelia
which make their way
towards the limits of the visible
at the same time your body
blindfolds itself
and stops its ears –
wanders through scattered streets
keen to delimit its mirrored back

Here the mental conflict is expressed as an aimless need for contact and a withdrawal. Mycelia were part of the underground metaphors of the day. For instance, one of the stories in Dorrit Willumsen's *The Hook* (1965) is called "Mycelium". Presumably betokening a latent feminism at the time. A sub-culture, before the women's liberation movement emerged in full flower in 1970.

Aimlessness found a different expression in another untitled poem by Kirsten Thorup:

Lost contacts
seem to consume
idle hours
sunless
motionless –
the humming bird is still

not circling –
like an excrescence
transplanted –
caught by the air
fixed in uncertainty

Contact is lost, movement does not move. The strange dynamism of uncertainty. If the poem is seen as a self-portrait, the
poet can be visualised, transplanted, fixing in suspense, transfor-
ming, motionless and yet in motion. Energy and beauty. Paradox. No one doubted that this was the start of an important body
of work.

It continued with *In Honour of the Occasion* (1968). Prose in
the coded language of modernism, without any definition of
genre: Kafka, Nabokov, Beckett had blazed the trail. Three stories, of which the first two, the account of a wedding entitled
"The Feast" and then the sketch of the day after, "The Bride's
Day", create the expectation that the third must represent a conclusion so that the book can be read like a novel. But that third
part is a story told in letters from a young patient in a nursing home
with only the odd mischievous link with the first two. Sadly,
these stories establish undefined, closed worlds with autonymous
workings which the characters in them have accepted and do not
even think of explaining more fully, for they live in them, but
which they nevertheless examine with meticulous care. The stories reflect a totalitarian power hierarchy with ritual wedding
feasts. The main character in the first has advanced from the
cellar to the auditorium and notes the events, torn within between past and future. On one occasion he has a note pushed into
his hand by some unknown person: "We meet in memory or
anywhere in Berlin." A promise? A threat? Or a maxim rather
like Kirsten Thorup's work in general? The second story is
viewed from the pinnacle of power, the point of view of the bride,
but it speaks strongly of a lack of contact and loneliness. Secret,
polite torture, the faint reflection of things happening elsewhere,
these constitute the shallow light in which the story is bathed. A
torn-off nail is kept in the jewel case of repression. Deeper feel-

ings must not evince themselves; they are sent their own subterranean ways. Mycelium. There is a clear hint of social awareness, not least in the third story which tells of a boy who loves writing and by means of this explores his own obsessive ideas, yet remains fixed in an absurd mythology which ascribes grotesque characteristics to the normal world surrounding him.

Kirsten Thorup was reflecting her own world in writing, but keeping within certain perfectly well-established literary patterns. Her poetry and schizophrenic prose helped her on her way. Let us take a parallel from the same period: In the 1960s Lars Norén wrote some poems from the tattered, multi-conscious world, which he referred to as "verbal remains of a vanishing pictorial splendour"; in 1968 came *Stupor,* containing a section entitled "Poems from the Carved Consciousness". There a footnote speaks of schizophrenia, but also points out that naturally this is not a book about sickness. The author refers his reader to Henri Michaux, who has spoken of "identity as a precarious balancing act between countless ego-possibilities, a mass in constant movement". One can go far in identification. It can be experienced as colossal expansion or catastrophic dilution.

Kirsten Thorup's next experiment after the intervening *Love from Trieste* was called *It's Daisy Today* (1971). The front cover represents a collection of glossy dolls which, despite slight variations, resemble each other closely. So does the array of characters in these short prose pieces which are rather like laconic poems or fragments of a story which refuses to be put together properly, a life pattern with combinations that will not fall into place. The characters are words in a linguistic game, interchangeable elements in an arbitrary syntax. In one passage M is curious to see whether she will be going to Trieste, as she has long wanted to do. Most of the episodes are centred on Bologna, or Venice, and a few other cities. They are like clips from an Antonioni film. M stands for Maria, one of Kirsten Thorup's preferred names. As time goes on, certain characters begin to reappear in her work, to wander from book to book. Sometimes they are identical, sometimes simply have the same names by coincidence. A modest modern counterpart to the idea Balzac practised in *La comédie humaine* of allowing old friends to reappear in later novels.

Sometimes Toni and Rita are brother and sister, sometimes lovers – though they do not love each other. Coordinates suddenly change to main and subordinate, in life as in syntax. Affluence and poverty are juxtaposed, and the characters change places and find themselves in conflict situations that are only registered on the surface. The soul is a series of abrasions and tiny itching insect bites. Here is the eponymous Daisy at work:

The beauty of rising at five in the morning, which we have
foisted on us
like in a forest the light can't penetrate like the urge to self-
preservation
when you have no money. You could cry over it
and go down into the street, it was suicide just as
it is impossible to sleep alone when you lie down
on the borderline between apathy and madness and
even if the bedclothes smelt of soap they could still
come sneaking up on you, those hyenas and the tiny
glazed figures of animals and Daisy had
black rings round her neck and she had not had enough sleep
and she let herself into the office building and took the lift up
she was to clean the offices before 9
she does the floors she does the waste paper baskets
she does the ashtrays she does the writing desks
she does the mirrors over the wash-hand basins she does the
washbowls
she does the toilets and she does the stairs

Women are attributed with the need to be objects and victims. We read of Maria: "She slowly crossed the road to give the cars a chance/ a chance to hit her and her legs a chance to be/ crushed and her head a chance to become a cranium. It had just been raining …". The motif reappears in *Little Jonna*.

That same year Kirsten Thorup made her first appearance as a writer of television plays with *The End of the Season,* a play about an artist couple who are leaving some town or other where they have spread confusion and bewildernment. It could be a day like Daisy. Or the day it was Harold Pinter. This was the start of a series of plays with a gradually increasing element of realism in the lunacy; on her way Kirsten Thorup took a look inside the walls of a mental hospital in her television adaptation of Amalie Skram's two novels about *Else Kant* (1978). It is about the subjection of women, consistently and paradoxically diagnosed as mental illness in a man's world. Her latest play is *Romantica* (1983). It is rather like a version of the book about Daisy, translated into terms of social realism and set against a background of desperate unemployment. An unromantic drama about the conflicts which the economic crisis is creating between people, with prostitution and murder as the result. The discoteque called Romantica offers but a brief consolation, as did the Mexicana Club in the first novel, *Baby* from 1973.

In this book two friends, Leni and Cadett are in town:

"'What are you doing afterwards?' she asked, and as she spoke her face became expressionless.

'I'm going to the bank', said Cadett in a melodious voice as though she had only learned to express even the most uncomplicated feelings long after growing up, and she took a bite of her bun, and she went over and took a newspaper that someone or other had left on a chair, and she quickly read through the column headed 'services offered – women' and 'services offered – men and women', and she did this every day; it was a mania she had, and she had a red dress and a black belt."

This use of "and" is known from the lengthy accounts of small children; the passage quoted contains the key to the way in which character is created in *Baby*. Cadett had only learned to "express even the most uncomplicated feelings long after growing up". But note that her voice has become melodious from this. This is the enchanting thing about Kirsten Thorup's babies that they are melodious in all their emotional poverty. There is an un-played music in their way of life, which is both conventional and rootless, but also inane. They have had experiences unknown to many adults living in protected worlds, but they cannot profit from them, adapt them, formulate them to give linguistic or existential coherence. But they can easily incorporate them into the remarks they exchange. They are not dull. Their melody is buried in the underlying tensions and conflicts, in the enormous sense of lack which conditions their lives.

This passage about the two girls is taken from the chapter called "The Financial Conditions in a Marriage", and indicates the inter-relationship between poor social conditions, lack of money and the emotions. Nowhere does the author embark on pedantic or didactic explanations of cause and effect. It is clear that the char-acters lack the conditions for growth, and that the way society is arranged is wrong. The parataxis has the effect of noting without commenting. She takes a bit of her bun instead of talking; she is going to the bank (to discover that she has overdrawn her current account), and she mechanically reads through the columns of "services offered – women" and " services offered – men and women", caught in the sex roles which no one can work out.

The quotation is only a sympton of how taut and carefully thought out the novel is; unostentatious as it is on the surface, nevertheless, without fuss, it pursues its fundamental themes throughout. The depth it contains is expressed in terms of glossy superficiality.

Baby is a collective novel without a collective. Almost all the characters are introduced in the first chapter in a Vesterbro bar called The Mexicana Club – Marc and Cadett and Leni and Susi and David and Nova and Eddy and Jolly Daisy. Then a few more are brought in in the following chapters and presented in various combinations of two's and three's as they experiment with as yet unestablished sex patterns – just as children cross the sex barrier at random. Because they are grown up now and have left child-hood behind, it all has the effect of the half-stifled revolt of misery against convention. And these are the worst conditions imaginable for revolution. "Tough guys" rhymes with "soft ice", and nothing useful comes from that combination. The stories of most of the groupings are taken up twice in the course of the novel, and it is made plain that there is no question of development, merely of a sequence of chance events leading to fresh problems. The formal end of the novel is betokened by the formation of a new couple, Leni, who is known from the first chapter, and the transvestite Jolly Daisy, who also appeared in the Mexicana Club. And Daisy begins to tell of her experiences. It's Daisy today. The characters move, but they stay in the same place. This novel plays a pivotal role in Thorup's work. The high degree of stylisation is on its way out. The narrator is ready and waiting just beneath the glossy surface, manifesting a restrained urge to reason. This novel is kept under impressively strict control throughout and represents the purest work of art Kirsten Thorup has created.

In the long novels following she frees her narrator and lets her break all rules governing points of view in fiction. The novels concerned are *Little Jonna* (1977) and *The Long Summer* (1979), in which the adult Jonna tells first of her childhood, when she was a 10-12-year-old, and then her early youth just prior to 1960. In the 600 page long novel *Heaven and Hell* (1982) the scene has moved from Funen to Copenhagen, and the young Maria is placed at the centre of a broad canvas of people and milieux. Only at a late stage does it emerge that Jonna is the omniscient narrator. Her brother John, who plays an important part in her childhood, now becomes Maria's husband. This little life has its vast open patterns.

Kirsten Thorup has an idiosyncratic approach to epic accounts. These books have the characteristics of realistic novels, the first apparently even being closely related to the author's own life as far as locality, social background and experiences are concerned. They are distinctly scenic and episodic, and the authorial stance can change abruptly if some character is to be considered in detail or introduced into the action from some time in the past. Dreams can be related, letters read aloud, diaries taken out, all in order to reveal aspects of people which are otherwise ignored.

Kirsten Thorup does not make use of the techniques and therapies of psychoanalysis to show how Jonna develops, but rather she makes use of her material to put an end to existential and social confusion. She takes emotional cross currents and turns them into a story. Thus the first novel about Jonna starts with: "When I was 10, my big brother was 21. I was terribly fond of him. And when I was frightened in the night I crawled over in bed to him." The retrospective distance implied by these words is gradually reduced until the narrator becomes identical with the girl she once was. Openness throws light on a world of modesty.

The emotions are treated more tangibly, more inquisitively, than is the case in novels of memoirs or of development written by men. This is how Aunt Marie is introduced: "Marie was an old maid, a little older than my mother. She had been engaged when she was 17, but had never married. And when I could not contain my curiosity and asked about her engagement, she smiled and looked down and said, 'That's my little secret.' And my interest in old maids stems from her." The same qualities are met again, for instance, in *Heaven and Hell* in the portrayal of the aging doctor's receptionist Miss Andersen, one of those grey and very ordinary people who on closer examination exhibit a huge range of unexpected characteristics, a labyrinth of human qualities which are laid bare with tenderness but not a trace of sentimentality.

This lack of sentimentality is a characteristic which I would in general venture to place alongside the matter-of-factness exhibited by women faced with unforeseen events and emotions. A calm ultimately springing from the echoes of an old peasant culture in the middle classes of today such as Kirsten Thorup has depicted them in the shape of the mother. She always has a proverb to suit the occasion. Behind this way of portraying her, which could be taken from a popular comedy, arises a proud and dignified figure; her calm can be undermined when doubt is cast on her honesty and sense of duty. This leads to depressions which increase in intensity towards the end of the novel. Nervous breakdown as a woman's fate.

In general the family does not enjoy good fortune. Indeed, things go seriously awry. The father is a farm bailiff, but is sacked and has to settle with his family in some rooms for the homeless before starting a life as a travelling salesman. It is in the 1950s, before the spread of affluence, and the little town near Middelfart shows a society in stagnation; the family can only look forward to a life of scrapping and scraping and humiliation upon humiliation. School, confirmation, a dance in the inn are all described as part of a life one would imagine belonged to more distant times. In *The Long Summer* Jonna has taken her middle school examination, but gives up the alien world of the high school. Apart from her, the family portrait centres in particular on her brothers: John is seen for a time as a circus hand who has his eye on the director's artiste daughter Daisy, while Verner comes home from New Zealand with Jane, whom he soon leaves. She and Jonna become friends, and we witness a number of charmingly intimate discussions between them of sexual problems. New perspectives are added to the story with Jonna's experience of seasonal work in a factory and a job in a mental hospital, which exercises a strange fascination on her thanks to its crazed inmates: "I have a definite reason for taking that job. I am convinced that at some time or other I shall end up in a lunatic asylum. I once thought I was on the verge of madness and that it was only a question of time before it would break out in me." Tiny motifs from the schizophrenic prose of *Daisy* turn up, for instance that of the man obsessed with turning on taps. Kirsten Thorup does not turn all taps on at full, but she uses her rich stock of material sparingly thanks to the same inventiveness and accuracy as Jonna shows when she has a job as a student in the Directorate of Trade Marks in Copenhagen – the third setting for this part of the novel, the office.

People live more than one life at a time. They are more than they are. The father, Carl Frederik's limited insight and ability to experience things emerges from the diaries which he nervously hands over to Jonna at the end – one of Kirsten Thorup's favourite short cuts to portraying character. She also uses this technique in *Heaven and Hell*, the vast portrayal of life in the Copenhagen of the 1960s. It is a broad account which is perfectly prepared to make use of the effects traditionally associated with the popular novel: chance but important meetings, the sudden inheritance of a million kroner, love at first sight. There is the strange saga of Miss Andersen, the receptionist, and in particular there is Maria, the daughter of a slum landlord and cigar-seller. She trains as a violinist, is gifted but principally driven on by her father's choleric ambition. Through her we experience the young people's revolt, the student movement, street demonstrations and confrontations with the police, but we see it from below, from behind, as a silent, slightly withdrawn spectator preoccupied with his own protest. Her mother is a witch with second sight, with whom at a late stage she achieves an intimate understanding.

The action is simple. Maria moves in with Jonni, who is a waiter and turns out to be bisexual; she leaves him and goes to live on a commune in Wales. She leaves hurriedly after a terrifying LSD trip, starts to play the violin in the streets at home in Denmark, and meets John, a taxi driver. Their marriage is founded on an uncertain economy. Can she go on with her training? Can he find a better job? This long novel has an open ending, with the couple planning to visit his family, among whom is Jonna, the sister with the literary gifts, the ironic narrator.

The book has been criticised by some as lacking in style, arbitrary in its composition, while others see it as an unique and sophisticated work of art. Presumably neither point of view is entirely correct. It reflects a mind concerned with heaven and hell, a richly contrasted mixture at once down to earth and distant, and containing razorblades packed in velvet, to quote a famous metaphor from *It's Daisy Today* – the book which after all is perhaps the most important and significant Kirsten Thorup has written. It expresses a tenacity and a black humour that goes right to the heart of this author's linguistic and existential qualities. There she says of M, i.e. Maria: "She never did more than one thing in a day. If she took the telephone she didn't eat that day. If she washed her hair she didn't speak to anyone for the remainder of the day. If she made some coffee she didn't read the women's magazines Toni brought home for her from the hairdressing saloon. If she went down and bought some rye bread and sugar she didn't watch television. If she had to hunt for the matches she didn't undress when she went to bed."

It is true, and it is the opposite of the truth. Surprisingly convincing and completely impossible. This is not the same Maria as the one in *Heaven and Hell*, and yet it is the same one. It is Kirsten Thorup. As "Kirsten Thorup".

Torben Brostrøm

Works by KIRSTEN THORUP:

Indeni – udenfor. [Inside and Outside]. [Poems]. Copenhagen: Gyldendal, 1967.
I dagens anledning. [In Honour of the Occasion]. [Short stories]. Copenhagen: Gyldendal, 1968.
Love from Trieste. [Love from Trieste]. [Poems]. Copenhagen: Gyldendal, 1969.*
Idag er det Daisy. [It's Daisy Today]. [Poems]. Copenhagen: Gyldendal, 1971.
Baby. [Baby]. [Novel]. Copenhagen: Gyldendal, 1973.*
Lille Jonna. [Little Jonna]. [Novel]. Copenhagen: Gyldendal, 1977.
Den lange sommer. [The Long Summer]. [Novel]. Copenhagen: Gyldendal, 1979.
Himmel og Helvede. [Heaven and Hell]. [Novel]. Copenhagen: Gyldendal, 1982.
Romantica. [Romantica]. [Play]. Copenhagen: Gyldendal, 1983.

*Published in English:

Baby. Tr. Nadia Christensen. Louisiana: Louisiana State University Press, Baton Rouge, 1980.
Love from Trieste. Tr. Alexander Taylor and Nadia Christensen. Copenhagen: Augustinus Forlag. Willimantic, CT: Curbstone Press, 1980.

SUZANNE BRØGGER

You Shouldn't Be Allowed
to Put up with It – !

by *Jens Kistrup*

SUZANNE BRØGGER (b. 1944) has lived abroad for several periods of her life (Thailand, Sri Lanka). Her frank and light-hearted attitude to the pleasures of life links her to writers such as Henry Miller.

Her work breaks down the traditional genres – essays intended to provoke discussion, interviews, short stories and books that can be classified as diary novels.

In the preface to her first book, *Deliver Us from Love,* the then 29-year-old Suzanne Brøgger wrote:

"The book is about the necessity and difficulty of jettisoning all our psychological and physical impedimenta. And so I have had to transform myself and reality in so far as it has been in my way. I have used myself for any purpose and to become anybody."

Suzanne Brøgger is stating a policy: This is what my work is all about. This is how I will make use of myself – not to say set myself up – as an author.

It is also a promise: This is my literary plan of action. This is the strategy I have devised for my life as a writer.

Against this background one must surely be allowed to observe that there are no surprises in anything that Suzanne Brøgger has written.

She is an author with a message. The political and feminist elements in her work are always subordinated to a greater cause. Or, perhaps, a loftier aim.

She has made herself the spokeswoman for a new and better way of living – in protest against everything that restricts or destroys human life: the nuclear family, marriage (monogamy), sex fixation – that conglomerate of love and sexuality found in both men and women but most especially in men.

"What there will be a need for in future is not specialisation, but generalisation: to be able to love more than one person, more than one country, more than one race, more than one sex – and not merely a single representative of the opposite sex."

On the principle of this revolutionary message she has told her own story – or at least one that could be hers.

There is the story of the hapless child who gathered sufficient strength to cope with life – including sex life – on her own premises. There is the story of a love affair from which it cost her an enormous struggle and a great deal of time to free herself

– because subjection or dependence were part and parcel of herself, indeed of all the impedimenta she brought with her from her European civilisation at this specific time.

These are the stories she tells in her two longest and best books, *Crème fraîche* (1978) and *Yes* (1984), which really have to be seen as novels in which the author plays the absolutely dominant role of principal character and heroine. But she produced pre-echoes of them in her first two books, *Deliver Us from Love* and *The Right and Wrong Paths of Love* (1975), both of which are a mixture of essay and short story, reflexion and documentation, autobiography and fiction with threads running back to the journalism which was Suzanne Brøgger's occupation for the greater part of a decade, before she became a "proper" writer.

There are examples of both reporting and interviewing in this dual début, in which Suzanne Brøgger apparently displays all her wares – obviously without having realised what literary ambitions she really had deep down inside her. Or perhaps they only developed later! While in *Deliver Us from Love* she is particularly keen to act as her own principal ideologist – supporting her argument with suitable case stories – *The Right and Wrong Paths of Love* clearly points the way to the books that were to follow.

For instance, the short story, "The Flower" – about a broken love affair from which it is difficult to escape – could well have been a chapter from *Yes.* The long interview with Mrs. Nynne, the milliner, entitled "You Shouldn't Be Allowed to Put up with It" is not only a presentation of the eponymous heroine of *Tone* (1981), but also of the principal motifs and some typical episodes from it. And the short piece called "Bacon" is a trial run at both the milieu and the characters in the portrayal of rural life which appeared a few years later under the title of *You Can't Roast a Pig That's Been Fighting* (1979).

Thanks to her sensational beauty – she is tall, impressive and sexy – and to her basic talent for placing herself in the limelight, Suzanne Brøgger has managed to create a public interest in her personality of the sort that is usually reserved for queens, multi-millionairesses, pop stars and film stars. She has turned herself into an act, with all the camouflage and mystery (for heaven's sake don't tell too much too soon!) necessary to sell yourself as a literary sensation and a provocateur in the field of (sexual) morals. And at the same time she has been able to supplement this image by the fact that at one and the same time she is at home in the international city milieu and has closer ties with the local Danish village scene than any other Danish writer.

The interest in Suzanne Brøgger as a phenomenon and as an author has doubtless been combined with an element of scandal and a good deal of confusion – there has been a tendency to praise her for those aspects of her work which have been least successful.

Then there is her less than harmonious relationship to the orthodox women's movement, whose explicitly and implicitly defiant attitudes she has refused to accept – at the same time as in one sense showing herself to be more radical and revolutionary than the women's movement has ever been, even in its most militant phase. This disloyal loyalty she herself made into the subject of an address delivered on the occasion of the 75th anniversary of the National Council of Danish Women, entitled "To Wish or Not to Wish".

For the crux of the matter, as seen through Suzanne Brøgger's eyes, is to wish to free yourself from "the old patterns and sexual codes with which we have been programmed, but which are becoming more and more unusable and claustrophobic". And the misfortune of women – including the feminists – is that in practice they have failed to carry through the liberation to which they theoretically have subscribed.

The fact that this liberation has been brought to a halt halfway is due to one single thing: fear of change. This is the reason for women's self-subjugation , for their fear of the unknown and the uncomprehended and the eroticism that frightens them more than death itself. And it is this fear with which Suzanne Brøgger's work takes issue throughout.

"The fear we all have of accepting that the old sex codes and behaviour patterns no longer apply. The fear of inventing new ways of life in acknowledgement of the fact that the old family life has lost its inner necessity. It is fear that explains why formal equality never becomes real equality. In the final analysis it is the fear of taking the consequences of being a human being and thereby of distinguishing ourselves politically from bacteria and insects and taking our libido and sexual urges seriously."

Suzanne Brøgger has remained loyal to this message. She has used it to provoke people – to provoke on many different levels, because on the one hand she has had to compete with the open discussion of sex in an age of pornography, and because on the other hand she has wanted to challenge the romantic concept of love (i.e. falling in love with and being faithful and devoted to one person), the positive sides of which she is probably inclined to dispose of too quickly.

It is as though there are experiences in this area which she has not had and curiously enough does not have the imagination to envisage. Is this the hapless child's real misfortune? But at no time has she revised or modified her universal utopia.

In this sense she is an author who says the same thing time after time. She has undergone an artistic development, but there is no development in the fundamental ideas she represents. Suzanne Brøgger has not debated these things even with herself, because there has been so much about which she has wanted to convince her surroundings.

Artistically speaking, however, she has progressed far from the basis of those two early books in which she first puts forward her point of view. In *Deliver Us from Love* and *The Right and Wrong Paths of Love* she sometimes seemed a little amateurish, uncertain of her methods. Even her humour at that time had a tendency to turn into nonsense. There is too much giggling in these books.

But then something happened. It was as though artistically speaking she took a firm grip on herself. She launched out into experiments which – though not totally successful – nevertheless made her burst her own bonds.

This applies to the quiet, everyday tone of her story of south-west Zealand village society, *You Can't Roast a Pig That's Been*

Fighting, which is certainly inspired by the desire to portray herself and her own life from a less "sensational" side, but which also approaches a view of death not as an enemy of life, but as part of life. And it applies to her at once most confident and most doubtful achievement as an author/poet, the epic called *Tone* – a poetical portrait of an earthly and ideal woman who lives and dies in the way in which, on the basis of the premises outlined above, Suzanne Brøgger herself finds it right to live and die.

Tone generously presents itself as "a woman's song to all those in need in needy times". But the idealisation in this vast prose poem seems on the whole overdone rather than convincing. It is as though readers are not allowed to see Tone with their own eyes, but in every single situation are kept in check by Suzanne Brøgger's lavish enthusiasm. All of this, however, has not prevented this epic – which is unlike most other things in Danish literature – from becoming Suzanne Brøgger's most consistent attempt at breaking new ground as a popular writer. Or is it perhaps only a poetical holiday from her role as the sophisticated lady of Danish literature?

Suzanne Brøgger is and has been a writer in the age of the media; the retrospective scrapbook called *Brew* (1980) clearly indicates her lasting links with freelance journalism, and it also contains her most profound analysis of Karen Blixen. Karen Blixen is otherwise visibly or invisibly present as a model or inspiration in most of what she has written. Even Suzanne Brøgger's handwriting looks as though it is fashioned on Karen Blixen's.

However, there has never been any doubt about her success in the media – despite the fact that a paradoxical shyness or reticence has made her a doubtful spokeswoman for her own points of view both on radio and television. But she is photogenic. She catches the eye.

It is well known that shyness is often identical with excessive self-assuredness. And Suzanne Brøgger is highly conscious of her own role as an author. This is apparent also in the unhappy love story in the novel *Yes,* in which one of the problems in the relationship between her and the anonymous obstetrician is the very fact that he finds it so difficult to accept her public posturing as an author. He thinks that she is consciously confusing people with her tomfoolery. But she has her defence ready:

"Yes, of course! That is my job. Authors always manipulate their readers, more or less openly. But the readers cooperate when they choose to be absorbed in the author's fictional world as though it were reality. They aim at a symbolical prize, but their stake consists in ignoring the author's manipulations."

And at least one equally significant trait in the author's make-up is related to this manipulative activity. That is his or her isolation. In Suzanne Brøgger's view it is impossible for an author to become attached to or dependent on anyone else. This is another reason why this love affair is doomed to destruction:

"I was entirely alone there, and there was no assent to be had. There was no one to give me permission. I could only take the law into my own hands if I dared. But the law wouldn't work if I associated it with praise or blame from any other person than myself. Did this mean that I was untouchable? It was a strange paradox that by writing I could reach out to others, but that I myself couldn't be reached. Suddenly I felt that I had violated some as yet unknown prohibition. Not that I had taken the law into my own hands, for you can do that – that I knew. But you must not initiate others into it."

To reach out to others without yourself being reached – this is no mean description of an author's role in general and of Suzanne Brøgger's in particular. It can be maintained that her entire talent as a storyteller and provocateur rests on a talent for constantly being at the centre herself and yet remaining untouchable, unreachable, not for those who would hold tight. Catch me, I won't be caught.

Her utopia is strictly speaking a philosophy of life for the very strong and triumphant – the nuclear family and monogamy perhaps afford greater protection and are emotionally easier to administrate than universal love, which it is so easy to transform into universal unfaithfulness and universal indifference. And throughout all its phases Suzanne Brøgger's ongoing account of herself in *Crème fraîche* and *Yes* – from a literary point of view the most significant books she has written – runs the risk of reducing all the characters in her life to a sort of secondary role. Even the man who, by her own admission, she was most in love with and with whom it was most difficult to break, is revealed rather than made intelligible.

The absolute quality of falling in love becomes a postulate. Passion is not seen as a vital or a natural force, but as an *idée fixe*, a whim as it were, of which for personal reasons and matters of principle it is a good thing sooner or later to be cured. How nice Suzanne – for you!

The conclusion must therefore be drawn that the basis upon which Suzanne Brøgger has chosen to become an author make her essentially different from other writers of women's literature today. On the other hand it has given her a freedom vis-à-vis both the political battle of the sexes and herself which artistically speaking has not only been an advantage but also a necessity to her.

In this respect *Crème fraîche* is the best and most sophisticated thing she has written – the absolute freedom with which she ranges over her own life in Denmark and abroad, and over her own past and present, has ensured this book a place as one of the major works of Danish literature in recent years. Irrespective of what objections people may otherwise voice against it.

Something similar can be said of the love story *Yes*, although it is mostly told in a completely different way. Here the exterior and interior drama is concentrated on two characters, of whom one is rejected, while the other is made intelligible – in a manner more reminiscent of advertising than of literature:

"I was completely indifferent as to whether what awaited me was pleasant or unpleasant, for my aim had always been to gain insight into myself and the workings of the universe. And so I had always said Yes to life, irrespective of the guise in which it appeared, irrespective of whether it came to tempt or to disturb, yes, yes."

In *Crème fraîche* there is a greater number of characters, although the same egocentricity or ego-fixation is present here as in almost all Suzanne Brøgger's work – though partly unconscious and never so direct that it develops into the conflict and the problem which one suspects it has been in reality.

In other words, there are aspects of herself which the tragic and triumphantly defiant Suzanne Brøgger has scarcely managed to touch on in her rejection of "love" and her affirmation of "life" – either because she has not wanted to or because she has not dared. Perhaps the next instalment will touch on that as well as on other things.

She has herself indicated her ambitious intention with her work at the end of *Crème fraîche:*

"I want to include EVERYTHING, I want to write about EVERYTHING, to clear a way through EVERYTHING."

Jens Kistrup

Works by SUZANNE BRØGGER:

Fri os fra kærligheden. [Deliver Us from Love]. [Articles]. Copenhagen: Rhodos, 1973.*

Kærlighedens veje og vildveje. [The Right and Wrong Paths of Love]. [Articles]. Copenhagen: Rhodos, 1975.

Creme Fraiche. [Crème fraîche]. [Novel]. Copenhagen: Rhodos, 1978.

En gris som har været oppe at slås kan man ikke stege. [You Can't Roast a Pig That's Been Fighting]. [Novel]. Copenhagen: Rhodos, 1979.

Brøg. [Brew]. [Articles]. Copenhagen: Rhodos, 1980.

Tone. [Tone]. [Poem]. Copenhagen: Rhodos, 1981.

Ja. [Yes]. [Novel]. Copenhagen: Rhodos, 1984.

*Published in English:

Deliver Us from Love. Tr. Thomas Teal. New York: Delacorte Press, 1976. London: Quartet Books, 1977.

DORRIT WILLUMSEN

I am only Afraid of Pure Angels

by *Bodil Wamberg*

In a small country such as Denmark we sometimes defend our artistic products by saying: If this novel, this play, this volume of poetry, had been written in one of the major languages, it would be world famous!

This kind of talk is at once defence and self-assertion. We would like to be world famous – and occasionally we have indeed succeeded in producing artists who have become just that. Yet at the same time we will also fight to the last drop of our blood to maintain our special character.

It also seems that the more outward show you put on in order to attract attention to yourself, the more you become identified with short-lived sensations and thus risk being forgotten or at best remembered as an excentric character who came one day and went the next. Yet authors, artists, really need great courage and strength to retire into the depths of their privacy, to shut everything out and simply surrender themselves to their creative urges and artistic fantasies. In that way there is at least no chance of being a short-lived phenomenon – but will such artists be discovered at all? It is terribly easy to be completely overlooked and left as the crank writer of countless unread books!

Here in our little Western European enclave we have examples of both attitudes. We know the strength of the silent artist when it springs from mysterious depths. But we have also learned the international custom of courting the market and the media by turning our lives into fairytale or myth. In particular with regard to this latter point, women have learned from men's professionalism.

Suzanne Brøgger and Dorrit Willumsen are two authentic representatives of these diametrically opposite attitudes. To begin with the one who is *not* the subject of this article, Suzanne Brøgger – she is in fact so brilliant as her own impressario, so adept at creating myths and legends about herself – not to mention the scandal she represents to the respectable middle classes – that she might well one day land in the very place at which she is obviously aiming: the top, in the full light of fame. Whether her talent will then last out is another matter, but outward appearance at least is something she has on her side: she

93

is tall and exceptionally beautiful – and she knows how to emphasise these qualities to the uttermost limit. Then she is apparently outgoing and prepared to tell everything about herself and her sex life (without really saying very much). She spends an inordinate amount of time talking about how lonely she is, and she invites endless streams of people out to her house in the country so that they can see for themselves how isolated and solitary she lives.

Not many people have visited Dorrit Willumsen in her home, which is also far out in the country. There she lives with her son and her husband, the big, wild and irrepressible poet Jess Ørnsbo. That is the limit of our knowledge. In reality we know nothing about her; she keeps entirely to herself and gives the impression that most of all she would like to hide herself away completely. She is very shy and reticent, and when you meet her face to face she is so diffident that you have to be made of cast iron not to be infected and appear to be just as diffident yourself. It is often difficult to get her talking; her conversation is hesitant and cautious and reveals little of her thoughts.

She seems delicate, small and fragile, as though the slightest breath of air would blow her over; she fascinates people, yet at the same time there is an aura about her which isolates her more effectively than any physical barrier. You instinctively hold back. Yet the last thing she can be called is affected.

If, on the basis of this description, the impression is formed that she is self-effacing, that, too, is wrong. In the midst of her shyness she is very conscious of her own worth.

I can best demonstrate something of all this by recalling one specific occasion. It was in 1981, and Dorrit Willumsen was to be presented with Denmark's most coveted literary award: The Danish Academy's Major Literature Prize. The ceremony took place as usual in the Academy's splendid old Copenhagen mansion in Bredgade one afternoon in November; a distinguished assembly of splendidly arrayed notabilities was waiting. On that same occasion, Suzanne Brøgger was to be presented with a smaller prize. Everyone had been invited for four o'clock.

I myself arrived early to make sure of a seat. It was empty and quiet everywhere – no one had yet arrived. Just one: the guest of honour, Dorrit Willumsen. She was quite alone in the great hall, standing in a corner and looking very pale. Her voice faltered a little, her hands were bluish and trembling visibly.

Time seemed almost to be standing still, but finally it managed to drag itself as far as four o'clock. All were in their places – waiting. For Suzanne Brøgger had not arrived. What had become of her? The air was tense, almost as tangible as a haze, a mist, that was becoming thicker and thicker.

Then, suddenly, there she was – a quarter af an hour late, of course. She made her entry, swept between the rows of seats with her swan-like neck held high – she was the Queen of Sheba.

As the recipient of the major award, it was Dorrit Willumsen who was to receive her prize first. It was presented to her with great ceremony. Then she made a speech of thanks. She spoke quietly, composedly and naturally. There was no sign of nervousness. There she stood on the rostrum, totally herself, entirely natural, neither self-assertive nor the opposite, but powerfully effective. It was incredibly quiet in the room; her audience sat in wrapt attention.

This episode reveals an essential feature of Dorrit Willumsen's way. The struggle takes place deep down inside her, in that totally enclosed world where she is alone. Her universe contains many kinds of fiction, but she does not embark on any kind of outward masquerading. Journalists cannot persuade her to perform on a tightrope; there is no dance of the seven veils on the screen.

Her way to the top has been long and difficult, but she has persisted, stubbornly, doggedly. Her first books were not read very much. It was said that they were too difficult, perhaps also too pessimistic. This was back in the times of economic expansion when the optimism reflected by the external situation was in inverse proportion to the pessimism of the general mood. Dorrit Willumsen is one of Denmark's few true female modernists.

Fundamentally, she has never written of anything but love – or, rather, the absence of love. She has constantly circled around the black hole of the feelings, which leads down to limitlessness, to the void. A life without love is the starting point for the many aberrant psychological states in her work: all sorts of depressions, schizophrenia, narcissism. Dorrit Willumsen has an expert's understanding of the mechanisms that cause people to misunderstand and misjudge each other. And this includes all kinds of relationships: between parents and children, between friends, both men and women, and between man and wife. Her women characters desperately cultivate their independence, reject their roles as wives and mothers, fail their children by simply leaving them in the middle of a park in broad daylight, fail their menfolk by changing their identity and becoming self-centred and sexless, man and woman at the same time. Or they start living like dolls or mannequins, soullessly moving through a progression of costumes, dresses, wigs and make-up.

And men flee for their lives. Or collapse beneath their depressions. Or seek some shelter in this mad situation.

Dorrit Willumsen covers a vast range in her excursions into inner and outer space. Her work sparkles with an infinite variety of style, settings and human types. She describes people in perfectly ordinary suburban settings, with their houses, cars, children – and all their conflicts. But suddenly she rises upwards, outwards, away from all everyday things, so her readers feel themselves transported to another planet. And she moves freely in time and space, back to ancient Rome, or forward to an electronically governed world of the future, in which people drive out in space on speedcycles or make love to robots.

In this vast universe the author speaks with many voices and in many tones. She creates a variety of moods, so that her readers are in turn moved, filled with horror and repelled. But sometimes they laugh, involuntarily, at the wild absurdities of life.

tea spice acrylic fee grasshopper is the title of the novel written in 1970, the year when the women's movement began in earnest. However, Dorrit Willumsen has always viewed a question from more than one angle and she has never been narrowly selfrighteous on behalf of her sex. One-sidedness has its own genetics.

The long ingenious alliteration pattern of the original Danish title *(the krydderi acryl salær græshopper)* gives the impression of complex, even confused, concrete concepts, but taken together they produce an abstract whole, and the symbolical values behind the individual concepts fall into place in a philosophy. Thus the novel becomes a modern, mythical fairytale about the birth and death of love. Historically it is the result of inherited family characteristics, and in the short run of a specific generation background.

The characters in the novel all base their lives and actions on petty obstinacy. The only and absolute aim in life for the spice merchant Camilla is to get her son Joachim to carry on the family tradition and become a spice merchant. Vanilla, cinnamon, raisins, nutmeg, are all the very essence of life to her – not to mention the really rare ones which make her long slender fingers tremble "as though she were standing before an aromatic poison". Her entire being is totally identified with her spices. Only tea is not to be found on the shelves of her shop, for tea was the downfall of her mother, who first killed Camilla's father with her endless variety of aromatic teas, and then herself became a tea addict.

One feels an immediate liking for Camilla, for everything she does is apparently so unusual and exotic that her actions are endowed with an aura of charm. For instance, she rubs the bedposts in her home with vanilla. And she is so absent-minded and helpless that there is always a pile of crumbs under her chair when she has been eating cake, while on the other hand she accidentally eats her serviette, which she has already been picking to bits in the heat of conversation.

However, it turns out that she is also dangerous, for at the same time she is supremely obstinate and a leech in her affections. Her son Joachim is afraid of her and in obedience to her wishes he becomes a spice merchant, although he is musical and ought to pursue his gifts in that field. In mute protest he develops a withered arm and then takes his revenge by compensating through a flourishing and exuberant love life with one beautiful Helene, who cares nothing for norms, money, welfare or fees.

Their lovers' nest is a tumbledown shack on the outskirts of civilisation, where Camilla refuses to set foot. "She dried up like a dark pod clasping bitter poisonous seed before it is blown away by the wind."

For many years all goes well between Joachim and Helene. Love really exists for them. In their tiny house there is grass growing on the doorstep and up through the floorboards; grass-hoppers and butterflies float around in these idyllic surroundings. All is peace and harmony until Helene's former fiancé Rasmus turns up and ruins everything by spoiling Helene and thereby causing her to make endless and unreasonable demands. This is too much for Joachim; a man who has developed a withered arm in protest has thrown away his chances of affording any effective opposition. So instead, he throws himself into the duckweed on the lake and drowns himself out of sorrow.

Narcissism and rancour thus creep in over the threshold of paradise and destroy it. Where does the guilt lie? And whose is the responsibility? They belong to both parties: to the weak (cowardly?) men who dare not defend their own identity. And to the monstrously sharp-tongued women who are determined to have their way – even if it results in the loss of limb and even life for others. This is the paradox: the more women prevail, the more they lose.

If the ability to survive is a sign of strength, then women are stronger than men in Dorrit Willumsen's work. Men are generally speaking well-intentioned and brutal, loyal and stupid. On the other hand, women's warped natures and psychological aberrations are of monstrous proportions.

The novel which was the occasion of Dorrit Willumsen's receiving the Danish Academy Prize, *The Man as Excuse*, is right at the centre of her poetical universe, for here she has concentrated all her experience of the conflicts between the sexes in her earlier work. The man, who is made the excuse for the women's lives, is placed at the centre. After all the battles for the women's cause in preceding decades, it is now first and foremost on his situation that our attention is focused.

We are not even told what he is called. He is *the man*, the

character-less man who is the product of society and what women make of him. He has no existence of his own; he is deeply
lonely and confused. Dorrit Willumsen has turned the tables:
whereas in the women's struggle it was a dogma that woman is
the victim of man, here she views the situation from the opposite
point of view. She portrays the man as the victim, as the excuse
for women's existence in general. They *use* him, as a provider, as
their dream hero, as the object of and outlet for their hatred,
their self-indulgence, their sense of being wronged. And they
pursue him from one to another, like a piece of wounded game;
he cannot satisfy anyone, either spiritually or physically, least of
all himself, however many wives or mistresses he might acquire.
In his powerlessness, his callousness and the brutality born of
desperation, he is almost traumatically compelled to bring about
misfortunes.

Finally, this man without identity dies a lonely and sudden
death in his car, his speed capsule as it is called, the symbol of his
restlessness and homelessness.

And no one misses him, for no one knows who he is or what he
wants to do with his life. When it comes to the point he is
superfluous, apart from his role as inseminator. Otherwise women can manage on their own.

No one loves anyone in this merciless novel, in which all
characters are narcissists. The place for love is vacant.

Dorrit Willumsen's most recent work is the long novel *Marie*
from 1983. It is not just *any* Marie who is at the centre of the
story, for this is a fictional biography of the life and art of Ma-
dame Tussaud. And this time it is the *woman* who is a traveller
through life; Marie is constantly on her journeys in England
with her exhibitions and wax models.

In a way it could be said that *Marie* is really the first novel
written by Dorrit Willumsen in support of the women's movement. But it is not an agitative novel in the normal sense. In it
she demonstrates that women can make a success of their lives
just as efficiently as men – if they *dare!* There is no end to the
challenges and struggles with which Marie is confronted. She
moves constantly and quite literally on the borderline between

life and death. The novel is set during and after the French Revolution, and in order to save her life Marie has to sit day after day in the Madeleine Cemetery and wait for the cart with the guillotined heads and dead bodies in order to make impressions of the faces of those who were important while alive. This is her task – she is forced to it. She has known many of these people, and some have been her close personal friends. So she has to turn away and vomit before, with superhuman discipline, she can compel her hands to obey her, first with the oil, then with the plaster mould for the mask. Then she models the faces in wax and exhibits them in her gallery. Such were and are the conditions imposed for working in a man's world.

In this terrible way Marie learns something about the distance an artist must maintain from the object to be represented, the artistic distance which is an absolute necessity in any process of artistic creation.

For Marie – and Dorrit Willumsen – *development* is the most important thing. However, the process of development is a terribly painful one; the price is high, both for oneself and for one's surroundings. One has to accept guilt and responsibility and it is impossible to avoid giving offence. Marie's last words, in her life and in the novel, are: "I am only afraid of pure angels".

In this she joins forces with Karen Blixen: Lucifer, the fallen angel, is her angel, for it is the fall from purity into the depths that gives an insight into human passions – and the ability to live.

Of course, Marie is not a typical woman, but with her life she gives expression to certain female potentials. Women, too, have creative abilities. But what about love? Where does that grow?

Only on one occasion does love have the last word in Dorrit Willumsen's fictional world. Paradoxically, it happens in the sinister world of robots and technology which she created in *Programmed for Love* (1981). In their manic search to do everything possible, to make everything function in their barren world of things and robots, men have also succeeded in creating a perfect sexual doll, the love robot Bianca. She can do all those things a normal living woman has not the energy to do in the long run.

Bianca is always at the height of her sexual capacity, she is always in a gloriously good mood, says the right things at the right times. In short she is man's banal dream of the ideal woman.

But of course, in time Bianca bores him to death. There is no reciprocity and therefore there can be no development. Bianca makes men even more lonely and isolated than before. Everything becomes hopeless to them.

There is only one way. The old one. The man and the living woman approach each other again, with all their problems and conflicts. They must try once more. Whatever developments take place in the world, they must try once more:

Slowly and gently
as over thin ice
the lovers approach
one another
They stroke the hoar frost
from each other's
shoulder.

Bodil Wamberg

Works by DORRIT WILLUMSEN:

Knagen. [The Hook]. [Short stories]. Copenhagen: Gyldendal, 1965.

Stranden. [Novel]. Copenhagen: Gyldendal, 1967.

Da. [Memoirs]. Copenhagen: Gyldendal, 1968.

the, krydderi, acryl, salær, græshopper. [tea spice acrylic fee grasshopper]. [Novel.] Copenhagen: Gyldendal, 1970.

Modellen Coppelia. [Coppelia the Model]. [Poems and Short stories]. Copenhagen: Gyldendal, 1973.

En værtindes smil. [Short stories]. Copenhagen: Gyldendal, 1974.

Kontakter. [Contacts]. [Poems]. Copenhagen: Gyldendal, 1976.

Neonhaven. [Novel]. Copenhagen: Gyldendal, 1976.

Hvis det virkelig var en film. [If It Really Were a Film]. [Short stories]. Copenhagen: Gyldendal, 1978.*

Manden som påskud. [The Man as Excuse]. [Novel]. Copenhagen: Vindrose, 1980.

Programmeret til kærlighed. [Programmed for Love]. [Novel]. Copenhagen: Vindrose, 1981.

Ni liv. [Short stories]. Copenhagen: Vindrose, 1982.

Marie: en roman om Marie Tussauds liv. [Marie]. [Novel]. Copenhagen: Vindrose, 1983.*

Umage par. [Poems]. Copenhagen: Vindrose, 1983.

*Published in English:

Complication. [From the collection *Knagen.* In: *The Devil's Instrument and Other Danish Stories*]. Tr. Paula Hostrup-Jessen. London: Peter Owen, 1971.

If It Really Were a Film. Tr. Ann-Marie Rasmussen. Willimantic, CT: Curbstone Press, 1982.

Marie. Tr. Patricia Crampton. [In preparation. London: The Bodley Head, 1986].

DEA TRIER MØRCH

A Journey in the Soul

by *Erik Vagn Jensen*

DEA TRIER MØRCH (b. 1941) studied at the
Academy of Fine Arts in Copenhagen. As a
lithographic artist she has concentrated on
simplified form in drawing figures.

She has a talent for characterising with a
minimum of strokes both as an artist and as a
writer. Most of her books are illustrated
throughout with her own linocuts.

L ate summer, 1968. The student revolt in France has subsided, General de Gaulle has achieved a convincing victory in the elections, occupied factories have been evacuated. Law and order prevail once more. The same is true of Czechoslovakia. After the summer's war of nerves between Moscow and the reform communists in Prague, the invasion came in August. Scarcely a shot was fired, but millions of fists were clenched in impotence, and millions wept. The Olympic Games were being prepared in Mexico, and there the black American sportsmen clenched their fists as they received their medals; "elections" were held in the Greece of the Colonels, and long-haired young people set out for their native lands after a long, hot summer.

Things were not quite so drastic in Denmark. Our Foreign Minister expressed support for the American war in Vietnam and explained that not only would it be breaking ranks with our allies, but also an unwise step to recognise East Germany. The "intellectual" daily newspaper *Information* discussed such topics as how much beer was drunk by grammar school pupils, the pressing need to allow the sale of LSD, and the appearance of red and black flags at a Grundtvigian Folk High School in Funen. And the poet Hans-Jørgen Nielsen fumed at the Danish Academy and described as an "aristocratic farce" the annual meeting of authors at Karen Blixen's old home of Rungstedlund. At the end of September rabies was confirmed on the border, and the weather was cool and damp. In other words, everything was as usual in Denmark.

Nor was the publication during these weeks of an illustrated book by a scarcely 27-year-old lithographic artist and painter, Dea Trier Mørch, much of an event for many people other than the artist herself. However, on the 28th September the radical newspaper *Politiken* carried a review of it of that rare kind which makes hundreds of readers open their eyes wide – and then go straight off to their booksellers. Dea Trier Mørch's book *Bitter-Sweet Socialism. Soviet Sketches*, the book about which Klaus Rifbjerg had written with such enthusiasm, was sold out in many shops that same day.

"Welcome, bitter-sweet young lady" was his title, and he went

107

on: "One has to be careful in using such terms as momentous debuts. I know. When you want to achieve the maximum effect you should express yourself in muted tones. All right, then I will speak in muted tones. Even so, I will predict in a penetrating whisper: If you have not heard of Dea Trier Mørch before, then you will do before long".

Dea Trier Mørch's impressionistic – or perhaps more accurately impressionistic *and* expressionistic – account of her travels in the Soviet Union was written after a period of study there. She calls it "a journey in the soul", and Klaus Rifbjerg's review compares it with two giants of Danish literature, Jens Baggesen and Tom Kristensen, whose accounts of their travels have become major classics.

We hear the gravel crunch beneath our feet, we witness great locomotives letting off superfluous steam, while from the kitchen we savour the smell of chicken soup and pirogi. The paint is peeling from the fences round the gardens of Novgorod; gently but firmly, Dea and her readers are led by militiamen away from the road where demonstrators are to march in a few minutes. We walk in the park with the babushkas in their worn shoes and enormous woollen shawls, and smile at doll-like soldiers from the country with red cheeks and blue eyes. We stand cheek by jowl with cosmopolitan painters filled with longing, and incomprehendingly sit face to face with neurotic bureaucrats.

We are in that vast, warm, absurd realm called Russia, the powerhouse of revolution and yet unchanged and unchanging. And our guide shows it all to us, pours out tea and vodka, shares her delight – and sadness – with us. One of the signs that the book is quite unique is the fact that the novelist Hans Scherfig bought numerous copies of it to give to friends about to visit Russia. He had been to the Soviet Union time after time and knew the official version through and through, but member of the Central Committee as he was, he preferred Dea's picture. Perhaps he did not agree with her on every point, but he regularly popped into his bookshop to buy a couple of copies.

Why did this young artist turn to writing? Because she felt so cut off in the vast expanse of Russia. And so she wrote letters, hosts of letters, to her family and friends. And when her good friend, the poet Ivan Malinowski, read about the mad Dutch swindler Victor (who is described in *Bitter-Sweet Socialism* and was not Dutch at all!), he gently coaxed her to write a proper account of her meeting with him, and with all the other people she had come across, and indeed of her meeting with Russia itself. And so she did. Ivan Malinowski set things moving, criticised her and encouraged her. And on all her travels Dea took Ivan Malinowski's volume of poems called *Forgetfulness* along with her in her luggage. A fount of inspiration on her travels.

But who was this young artist? The best impression can be gained from reading her books. Nevertheless, we can here say that Dea Trier Mørch was born on the 9th December 1941 in Copenhagen as the daughter of an unmarried woman who a couple of years later also produced a son. This mother, Ibi Trier Mørch, was an architect, and as time went on she did a few hours a week teaching industrial design at the Academy of Art. Together with her two children she lived in a small flat in Nyhavn in the centre of Copenhagen; they had few possessions, but they had many relatives and friends. Most of these people, architects, town planners, artists and educationalists, held left-wing and sometimes socialist views. And then there was another group made up of Ibi Trier Mørch's excentric relatives from the area around Vallekilde Folk High School in the west of Zealand. Ibi's father was an honest civil servant, while her mother, a most unusual person, was a self-trained artist. Dea Trier Mørch's novel *Chestnut Avenue* (1978) paints a vivid picture of them; it is admittedly a novel, but nevertheless, the three siblings in the book share many features with Dea and her brother. And as in other novels by Dea Trier Mørch, the "missing father figure" is sensed in the background, but is held at bay by an array of noisy and fond relatives.

Dea Trier Mørch's maternal great-grandparents were the first principal of Vallekilde Folk High School, Ernst Trier, and his wife Julie Marstrand. Descended from immigrant German Jews, he was now assimilated, baptised and an enthusiastic spokesman for the special Grundtvigian form of Christianity with its aim of enlightening ordinary people by means of history, Nordic myths and poetry. The characteristic Folk High School tradition, understood by few outside Denmark, together with a Jewish sense of family and background, have made their mark on Dea Trier Mørch.

Little Dea grew up as a conscientious and loving big sister. She talked and drew a lot, was wise beyond her years and had a lively imagination. When she went to school she turned out to be dyslexic. She was sent to a special school and learned mnemonics and other practical systems: vowels are red and consonants black. She learned to keep things tidy and tried to understand things that were difficult and demanded precision. She embarked on a systematic attempt to overcome her handicap! Of course you can do it! Write it down, Dea, and then repeat it! You'll get it in time.

This "handicap" and the determination to overcome it – plus her immediate environment, her relatives, her "missing" father, the family tradition and the family feeling – all are easily recognisable in Dea Trier Mørch's five novels.

She went to school for ten years and at the age of sixteen was offered a place in the Academy of Fine Arts – without an entrance examination. The work she had done in her spare time was sufficient. In those days "abstract" painting was the fashion, and she studied it under Egill Jacobsen. But she did not actually *learn* very much. She was eager to introduce order into her thinking, to see relationships, to be taught, but all these things were done outside the Academy. Then she began to be active in the students' representative council in order to meet with some challenges; at the age of 18 she was elected chairman of the council, after which it was natural that she should be elected to the committee of the Council of Danish Students.

Just as in her family and at school, Dea was met with trust and kindness everywhere. Everyone concerned with her was always convinced that the challenge and the tasks were something which the lively and inquisitive Dea could easily manage! And she did.

As for politics, she did not belong to any party, but she was out to the left of centre in her views. Then, about 1960, she went to Poland to attend a meeting of students at Gdansk, and she discovered that *that was where things were happening!* Despite all the political difficulties, despite censorship and divisions between people, the posters on the walls were exactly as they should be! And the poets wrote, and the painters painted, and there was a flourishing confusion of madness and talents and tiny theatres.

When she came home and was still poor, she discovered that she could apply for scholarships to study in the socialist countries. They would not provide her with vast sums of money, but they were enough to live on. And to learn something. Something systematic, something different from what she was doing in Copenhagen.

She spent eighteen months in Poland, six in Yugoslavia, a year in the Soviet Union and three months in Czechoslovakia. She learned languages (mainly Polish), read literature (including the classics of socialism), found friends and received instruction in the schools of art, learned new techniques of, for instance, etching in Leningrad and linoprinting in Prague.

And then she began to write books in earnest.

In 1970, two years after going into print for the first time, she published a related though naturally entirely different book about her impressions of Poland.

Again we are in the company of a Dea with eyes wide open and a sketchbook in her hand. We visit Krakow, the old sepia-coloured Habsburg city, the rebuilt capital of Warsaw with its sweeping avenues and outsize houses built on the rubble, and with the forbidding and fascinating Hotel Bristol which the Germans forgot to raze to the ground. We see the Baltic cities, also newly rebuilt with their cathedrals and historical warehouses reconstructed exactly as they were before the war; we are given a glimpse of villages right over by the border with White Russia. And we are surrounded by the idiosyncratic, artistic and ungovernable Poles.

Both these "travel accounts" are written in a style completely different from that in Dea Trier Mørch's later work. There is a host of associations, long tripping sentences, and romantic history. Perhaps she does not always *know* everything, but boldly and intuitively she describes things as they really were in such a way that her account often rings truer and profounder than many presentations by professional historians – even if they have a hundred times as many source books as this inquisitive artist.

Even before the publication of *Poland* (1970), Dea Trier Mørch, together with Thomas Kruse and other friends and fellow artists, had founded an artists' collective called "Red Mother". Those taking part in the experiment were lithographic artists, people connected with the theatre, and musicians; most of them were Danish, and as time went on most established links with the Danish Communist Party. One, the Japanese artist Yukari Ochiai, was one of Dea's friends from the Leningrad school, and although she had only spent a couple of short periods in Denmark she played an active part in the collective's general attempts to create a "proletarian" art relevant to modern conditions such as could be *used* by the working classes and politically committed youth. Many of the graphics and posters produced by Red Mother were collective efforts not bearing the signatures of specific individuals. It dit not, however, mean that the individual artists could not also exercise their independent skills. From 1969 onwards, Dea Trier Mørch illustrated a whole range of important books by, among others, Georg Trakl, Vladimir Mayakovski, Pablo Neruda, Ivan Malinowski – and Marx and Engels (The Communist Manifesto).

In 1972 Dea Trier Mørch came to the conclusion that as a result of her experiences, her reading and her desire to help change the conditions of the world and of mankind, she must join the Danish Communist Party. Her membership lasted for ten fruitful though by no means unproblematic years. She left the Party in the spring of 1982 without reacting in the way of so many other disappointed former communists. She had known an inspiring comradeship in the grass roots of the party, but she reacted against the stiffness and the centralism in the party apparatus, the unwillingness to change and the absence of the ability and will to learn from present-day concrete reality so as to review their style and their everyday approach to politics to gain the trust of the Danish people.

Then Dea Trier Mørch became a mother. During the 1970s she

112

and the painter and musician Troels Trier had three children. This experience of giving birth to three children within four years had a decisive impact on her life. She wanted to give artistic form to her experiences, to tell of them, ask others, write a book about the miracle which a birth is. In 1976 she published *Winter Children* in Danish. Since then it has had hundreds of thousands, indeed millions, of readers in Norway, Sweden, Iceland, Greenland, Finland, Holland, East and West Germany, Switzerland, France, Italy, Portugal, Yugoslavia, Hungary and Poland. There was a need for this book.

Winter Children, Dea Trier Mørch's greatest popular success so far, is a collective novel about eighteen women and their social and family backgrounds. They are all in the maternity ward of the National Hospital in Copenhagen in the weeks around New Year 1975. The other characters in the novel are the "patients'" husbands, children and other relatives, together with the cleaners, auxiliaries, nurses, midwives, doctors and consultants working in the hospital – and all the newborn children. There were many who expected that this writer, who was known for her social criticism, would hit out at the hierarchy, but on the contrary, the book is an expression of homage to the people working in a large hospital.

The women who have been sent there to have their babies come from different classes and environments, and some of them will be discharged to return to difficult, demanding and probably cold family relationships in which they will be left almost entirely to their own devices. But in the hospital they belong together, they have things in common, they are aware of the care – and of the solidarity – of their sex.

This novel is written in a sober language, and the sentences are short. The great questions of life and death are discussed in subdued tones. It created such a powerful impression that scarcely anyone ventured to criticise the consciously muted language. On rereading now, one might well feel that it is just a little too disciplined, that just a little carefreeness might have been a good thing.

As has been said, *Winter Children* has been published in many countries – and likewise in all kinds of editions, hardback, paperback, book-club. And only a year after publication it was filmed by Astrid Henning Jensen. It was given its first showing on the same day in all the Nordic capitals, even in Nuuk in Greenland. Since then it has been awarded prizes in international film festivals and has been shown in cinemas and on television in East and West alike.

As a result of this book Dea Trier Mørch got on to first name terms with her many readers and became known as Dea. She was in constant contact with countless people through letters and lecture tours, readings and discussions, first and foremost in Scandinavia, but subsequently also in other countries in Europe. She scared Christian audiences in Norway and shipyard workers in East Germany by smoking a pipe and saying shocking things without wrapping them up in conventional phrases; but they ended up by liking Dea a lot.

In 1978 the novel *Chestnut Avenue* was published, illustrated, like the rest of her books, with Dea's own linoprints. Maja, Martin and Malthe spend a summer at their grandparents' home in a village in central Zealand. We are in 1948, and as has already been indicated, there are quite a lot of points of similarity with Dea's own childhood. The family background is Grundtvigian, influenced by the nearby Vallekilde Folk High School. The house is full of pictures and books, drawers full of strange things, dark corners and attics. In the stable there are pigeons, poultry and cats. In the gardens fruit trees and old-fashioned flowers. The grandfather represents the established moral system, while the grandmother, thanks to her humorous and sometimes coarse comments is constantly in opposition. Under the influence of the resultant interplay between the grandparents the children's awareness is fashioned. In the winter the seven-year-old Maja is left alone with the elderly couple, and consequently comes to be even closer to them.

In this book Dea Trier Mørch shows that she has a feeling for the Danish countryside, that she remembers what it was like to discover the world as a six or seven-year-old. Her novel is a storehouse of observations of animals, plants, weather, people

and things. Of tastes and smells, of delight and fear. Some reviewers accused it of being pure nostalgia and idyl, but they
failed to notice the sense of dread that also lurked in this childhood summer with its stories read aloud in the light of the lamp,
its stewed fruit, its cuddles and its late nights. The father is far
away, in a sanatorium. And fear makes itself felt at the end of the
lane in the poor house with its worn and bent inhabitants; they
allow Maja to hold their tiny child – and she drops it on the
cobblestones.

In general, however, it is an optimistic book about the way in
which the old and the very young get on together well away from
the watchful eyes of parents.

By contrast the next novel *The Inner City* (1980) is about
children and their parents. It takes place in Copenhagen during a
fortnight in August 1979. The principal character is Lulu, whose
husband Danny is active in both his trade union and the Danish
Communist Party. He is highly respected by his workmates,
works for his class and his party – and not unnaturally is sometimes rather tired. Lulu stays at home to look after their two
small children, one of whom has just started school. She, too, is a
member of the party, does her duty collecting money, selling
newspapers, going to study groups and parents' meetings in the
nursery school, bringing up the children – and is very tired.
And the conflict between the demands made on her from the
outside and her own personal needs, the sense of being entirely
alone with pressing problems, the lack of close personal contact
because there is so much else to be attended to, those things it is
her duty to do for the great cause – all this is the subject of this
novel. And it is about desperation and Lulu's sense of loneliness
despite her friends and despite the aims which she shares with
Danny. And it is about the beginning of a revolt against a situation which is intolerable for two young people who are fond of
each other and of their children. There is no need to be a communist to feel the truth of this book!

Some people complained of the unadorned language in *The
Inner City*, but this is compensated for by the warmth with
which the characters are portrayed and the fond picture of central

Copenhagen. There is perhaps just a touch of exaggerated didacticism in the many explanatory comments, reasonable and correct as they all are. But there is no universal recipe for how the young mother and her husband ought to organise their lives. There is no patent solution. It is rare to see a family depicted with such insight, understanding and love, and the children's language is absolutely authentic. In fact, weighty as are the problems treated in Dea Trier Mørch's novels, they are also *fun* to read – not least because of the children in them.

Dea Trier Mørch's life underwent many changes during these years. In 1979 she was divorced and left alone with her children. The following year her mother died after suffering long from cancer – in Dea's home.

During that time incredible demands were made on her, and the death of her mother came understandably as a great relief. But all those things she had thought and *dreamt* of in all those months, all her reflections and self-reproaches, had to be worked through and matured so that she could get on with living life for herself and her children.

The result after almost eighteen months of work and five revised versions was the novel *The Evening Star* (1982), which also turned out to be a much-needed help to countless readers in Denmark and abroad.

It tells of the dying Bett's last nine months together with her son Niels Peter. It is about love and demands for love, first and foremost between these two. And about the course of an illness, its treatment, the drudgery resulting from it – and about everyday life with the children, the family and Niels Peter's fiancée. The last part of Jens Kistrup's review in the daily newspaper *Berlingske Tidende* sums it up as succinctly and sensitively as it is possible to do:

"*The Evening Star* is, then, at once a very private, indeed profoundly personal novel about the great forces with which we are confronted: life, love and death – and also a novel with what might be called a political significance. And it slowly works its way forward to accepting the death which brings separation and

116

obliteration, and which it is almost impossible for us to face. Is it not the significance of death that we must make way for others?:
'The dead person makes way for others. And what we have shared with her or him – intimacy, love, anger or possession – has now to be shared with others. We have to learn to give our feelings a new direction and to make use of each other in a different way. The baton is passed on to the next runner'.

So vast and so difficult is the perspective in this novel by Dea Trier Mørch, a book at once immensely banal but also immensely significant and relevant to modern experience. It is no coincidence that the son Niels Peter wishes that we had a producer who could show us our right places on the stage, formulate the highest ethical common factor and shoulder the responsibility. But how many of us have such a person who can give guidance – political, ethical or religious? There is certainly none for Bett, as she approaches death, or for her children. They have to cope with the illness on their own, the sorrow, the loss, the funeral and the reception afterwards for all their friends. Death is seen as a part of life. Perhaps the most difficult part of all.

In *The Evening Star* Dea Trier Mørch in one sense completes what she began in *Winter Children*. Together they centre on the beginning and the end of life – which is also the condition for its continuation. She has brought all these things almost as vividly to our attention as it is possible to do. It is impressive, and indeed much more than impressive."

Dea Trier Mørch's latest novel is *The Morning Gift* (1984). It is at once a novel about a modern marriage and a study of the artist's predicament.

It begins in 1968 in Copenhagen with an intense love affair. She, Signe, is 30, and he, Jacob, is 40. They miss each other terribly when unreasonable and irrelevant factors such as work separate them for a few hours; they meet in exuberant happiness, dance through the city's parks, deliberately prolong their walk home to bed so as to extend the delight of anticipation. All colours become bright, and things around them feel completely new to the touch; everything is experienced as never before.

Seldom in Danish literature has love been depicted with such sensuous intensity as here.

They are both ceramic artists, move out into the country, marry, love each other and have four children within eight years. Their working lives and their family life are described, as are the children's development (and Dea Trier Mørch *knows* what children think and say!), birthdays and Christmasses, and the light dances over the countryside.

But Signe is more successful in her art than he. She exhibits and meets with acclaim – and jealousy! In order to maintain a natural relationship, including the sexual relationship, between them, in which he gives and protects, she has to keep a firm grip on herself. She has to play a background role and continue her own personal and artistic development without being noticed.

For long periods when the artistic creative process demands everything of Signe she tries to avoid marital relations in bed. She asks for a pause, a little respite from her "marital duties" in order to live on the other level, the level of artistic creation. Sublimation.

But Jacob's powers of understanding are not sufficient. He is too selfish or perhaps too stupid. And so the relationship between them breaks down, little by little, despite their many attempts to reestablish it. In the long run it cannot go on – despite four children and despite all the good qualities Signe can see in her demanding – and generous – husband. It ends with a "happy divorce".

There are fewer authorial explanations, fewer fingers pointing the direction in this novel than in the four earlier ones. More is left to the reader. But in the other books Dea Trier Mørch wants to throw light on the serious problems of life as she and others experience them in our time. She also wants to teach her readers something, to show them what she has seen and thought through. She is writing a didactic novel. A few, but only very few, readers are irritated by the many excellent explanations of the problems encountered, but in real life there *are* usually good explanations of this kind. Though we tend only to discover them when it is too late.

Behind Dea Trier Mørch's book lies a search for a philosophy of life, a desire and a will to discover a coherence in life. And there is also an impressive amount of hard work, indeed a unique example of working things together.

Although she is deeply inspired by marxism, she has throughout been concerned with the transcendental. She has felt a link with something in nature, felt that in certain situations one suddenly achieves a profound insight. It is the first experience that is most important, not its – trivial – repetition. When you seek something with sufficient concentration, you have a sudden experience – it is like a gift – all is clear; you have crossed a boundary. Dea Trier Mørch often speaks of *crucial* experiences, the decisive ones. Experiences in which you receive signals and sense somthing great, almost divine. The Christian concepts like grace, forgiveness and reconciliation, and the socialist ones like solidarity and fraternity are perhaps in reality fundamental common human concepts. For Dea Trier Mørch Grundtvig's words that "man is of spirit" and the desire of socialism to distribute material goods equally have been quite decisive.

Meanwhile, I cannot conclude this attempt at presenting Dea Trier Mørch and her writing without saying something of how she works. When the plans for a new book are beginning to take shape in her head, it has been known for Dea to ask her publisher to put aside a day for an initial discussion of the idea. Not an hour or two, but a whole day. I can confirm this, for I have experienced it.

It has, for instance, taken the shape of a long morning walk in the Deer Park, followed by lunch in an inn nearby, while the rest of the afternoon saw fresh jugs of hot coffee on the table at regular intervals. She has talked for half hours at a time and then asked for a reaction to what she has been saying. We have discussed things, disagreed sharply on details, argued in a friendly way, and when darkness has fallen we have taken out our diaries and arranged to continue the battle another day. Then comes the first version. The publisher receives a second version in Week 10, and the following Monday is set aside for a careful consideration of the manuscript, page by page. A new version is ready in Week

19. Copies sent out to friends and professional readers. The corrected manuscript to the publisher 26 days later. Perhaps time for a new version of certain passages; it can just be done, and it is noted in Dea's diary. New discussion days are arranged. Illustrations ready for submission, lay-out, making up etc. New dates.

No, it is impossible to give a realistic picture of the genesis of Dea's manuscript, but I can guarantee that she is not one of those stubborn authors who simply submit a finished manuscript and tell their publisher to get on with it!

Her background – and view of life – do not allow that.

Erik Vagn Jensen

Works by DEA TRIER MØRCH:

Sorgmunter socialisme. Sovjetiske raderinger. [Bitter-Sweet Socialism. Soviet Sketches]. Copenhagen: Rhodos, 1968.
Polen. [Poland]. [Travel book]. Copenhagen: Rhodos, 1970.
Vinterbørn. [Winter Children]. [Novel]. Copenhagen: Gyldendal, 1976.*
En trekant. [Short story]. Copenhagen: Brøndum, 1977.
Ind i verden. [Handbook]. Copenhagen: Gyldendal, 1977.
Kastaniealléen. [Chestnut Avenue]. [Novel]. Copenhagen: Gyldendal, 1978.
Den indre by. [The Inner City]. [Novel]. Copenhagen: Vindrose, 1980.
Aftenstjernen. [The Evening Star]. [Novel]. Copenhagen: Vindrose, 1982.
Morgengaven. [The Morning Gift]. [Novel]. Copenhagen: Vindrose, 1984.

*Published in English:

Winter's Child. Tr. Joan Tate. [In preparation. Lincoln: University of Nebraska Press, 1986].

ELSA GRESS

A Resoundingly
Well-integrated Troublemaker

by *Mogens Knudsen*

ELSA GRESS (b. 1919). Within the space of three years she made her appearance as an essayist (*Incursions*, 1945), dramatist (*If*, a play for radio, 1946) and novelist (*Interlude*, 1947).

Elsa Gress is an active critic and she has written many articles, also in American journals like *Drama Review* and *Leonardo*.

She has been awarded numerous important prizes and since 1975 she has been a member of The Danish Academy.

S he is an author in the fullest sense of the word. She lives by her pen and spans almost every literary genre: novels, short stories, dramas, memoirs, essays, journalism. Poetry accounts only for a limited amount of her writing, but there are nevertheless songs in her plays, and she has published a volume of her own verse recreations of internationally significant literature both old and new.

And she is ready to make use of all the media by means of which a writer can establish a channel of communication with the public at large – books, theatre, films, articles in newspapers and magazines, radio and television, lectures and discussions. Thanks to her wide interests and her reluctance to leave unsaid whatever she happens to think of any conceivable subject, she has established herself as a central figure in the public discussion of a wide range of subjects of topical interest.

Elsa Gress is a literary historian by training, and before completing her M. A. in 1944 she was awarded a gold medal for a dissertation on the emergence of classicism in English literature. An academic career was obviously open to her, but she was not attracted by it. As an active participant in the Resistance movement, she was living underground when she took her final examination, and when, after the war, it again became possible to travel abroad, her restless nature and her thirst for experience moved her to embark once more on the visits to foreign countries she had undertaken on very small means in the late 1930s. She went to England – which she found exciting and exhilarating despite the ravages of war – and later won a scholarship to the U.S.A. There she wrote a number of critical articles in the Danish press, with the result that she was expelled from the U.S., a country which had always fascinated her, but for which she had always had mixed feelings.

The time she spent abroad has had its repercussions in her life since. She married an American, the painter Clifford Wright, and has three children. At the beginning of the 1960s they moved first into a former village school in southern Zealand, and later into a house belonging to the manor of Marienborg on the island of Møn where they have developed an informal set-up which has become not only the framework round an active family life, but also an open house for Danish and foreign writers, actors, painters, musicians and dancers. It grew into a very informal institution by the name of Decenter.

Elsa Gress has chosen the life of an independent artist with all its possibilities and all its financial insecurity in preference to a safer way of life with a more limited potential. She has not done so, however, without complaining bitterly that the modern welfare state treats its artists badly, especially those who are off-beat, imaginative and innovative. Far too often they come up against a wall of establishment respectability in the shape of commissioners, secretaries and officials with authority in the agencies established to further culture and the arts, and in the persons of permanent reviewers with permanent opinions, theatre managers, publishers, representatives of radio and television, government and local authorities. They have the powers but seldom the understanding – as she is not slow to point out.

Although her work takes many different forms, there is a unity about it. She is both a critic *and* an artist, and does not herself feel that the two approaches make conflicting claims on her. The same things can be said in different ways.

Her first book, *Incursions* (1945), is a modest collection of literary and academic essays, most of them written while she was still a student. However, the preface outlines a policy in which she says that although there is no cohesion in the points of view in the individual essays, they have in common what could be called critical idealism, the belief that the negative has the right to exist alongside the positive, and the conviction that respect for "impractical" ideas and studies is a necessary precondition for all culture in a broad sense.

This view has been a permanent feature of all she has written: she regards criticism as a basic form of literary expression, as is quite obvious in so far as a degree of criticism constitutes an integral part of most artistic creation, while on the other hand a sense of artistry is indispensable to all good criticism.

Talented, vigorous and determined, Elsa Gress has asserted the importance of the art of criticism as a creative literary common denominator. There will always be differences in quality, but "creative writing" will not necessarily give a deeper insight into life and human nature than reasoned argument. A consistent personality asserts itself irrespective of genre. For instance, in her novels as well as her memoirs she maintains a balance between sensitivity and intellect, between narrative and interpretation. As an example of how the relationship between the two kinds of writing is misunderstood she criticises the cataloguing system used in Danish public libraries, according to which memoirs are classed as non-fiction, whereas they ought rightly to be included together with novels and short stories. A more appropriate classification of memoirs would moreover mean that reviewers and readers need no longer express pointless surprise at the inclusion of autobiographical elements in works of fiction or poetry, or at the presence of imaginative elements in autobiographical publications.

A figure constantly recurring in Elsa Gress' early novels is a young, insecure, intellectual woman who has features recognisable from the author's own life and from what she later relates about herself in her memoirs.

Interlude, which was awarded a prize on its publication in 1947, is a typical postwar novel reflecting the narrator's first visit for seven years to a now bomb-scarred London. She is in a state of uncertainty, unsure about her own future and a prey to recurring fits of depression brought on by her memories of unpleasant experiences in Denmark towards the end of the war. The course of her life has been disturbed, and a brief love affair in which the emotions are not involved fails to reconstitute her. She only gets on close terms with very few of the many people whom she meets and with whom she engages in dispassionate discussions about Freud and the neo-Freudians, the Russians, the Americans, modern philosophy, marriage, divorce, hungry Europe and the danger of a new war. She has the alert senses of a young woman, to the benefit of her descriptions of the mood in London, and as she leaves for home she is sent on her way with some words of encouragement from one of her true friends who has been through the Spanish Civil War: "I am a pessimist, but let me tell

127

you that it is not what you experience that is essential. The important thing is to give the right expression to your experience. You want to write. Well then, write. Fight. You have to live and use your life. You know that perfectly well, but I am saying it so you won't forget."

Liz is the name of the Danish girl in *Concertino* (1955), an ambitious experiment, a group novel in which a handful of people all aged around 30 find themselves together for a few weeks as they take part in an American-European seminar held in a baroque palace in Austria five years after the end of the war.

The characters represent various countries, and some of them have directly experienced the war on one side or the other. Points of tension emerge between the Europeans and the Americans, several of whom feel like fish out of water. However, the characters are not there merely to voice opinions. Behind the formulation of the ideas and attitudes inculcated in them one senses personal doubts and difficult emotional complications.

If all this seemed somewhat spartan to the traditional reader of fiction, the next novel, on the other hand, offers all they could wish for in the way of love story, warmth and imagination. *The Earth Is No Star* (1956) is the story of Judith who has gone to the United States to study and also to re-establish contact with Bob, whom she has met at home in Europe and with whom she has fallen passionately in love. However, he is married and is anything but exciting when on his home ground. To the detriment of Judith's studies and peace of mind her love only leads to a condescending apathy towards Bob, but at the same time it gives rise to bitter scorn for American family hysteria and the nightmare of conformity to which intellectuals are especially subjected in the age of McCarthyism.

The love affair with Bob leads to complications. Judith is pregnant when she has to leave for Denmark earlier than planned because she is refused an extension of her residence permit. And with a mixture of tenderness and irony this child of hers now becomes the focal point of the action. Out there on the star inhabited by the unborn it is bored and keeps watch on the two it has chosen to be its parents. Totally indifferent to the awkward situation ensuing and the difficulties facing the ill-matched couple, the potential child urges its parents-to-be to get together and multiply so that it can be born and admitted to the playground and battleground known as the Earth, which happily is no star.

When this novel was first published it was seen in certain circles as a traditional piece of anti-Americanism, though this is not the case. The love story is the essential ingredient, the arrival of a new human being with roots in both the old and the new worlds. Naturally a liberal-minded young Dane was bound to react in some way or other on her first encounter with the U. S. in 1951, but just as naturally she was bound to modify her views as a result of many occasions on which she renewed the acquaintance. She has been accused both of anti-American sentiments and of being uncritically favourable towards America. She herself says, "What I particularly love about this gigantic, open society is precisely its generosity, its wealth of possibilities, despite everything and because of everything. – In contrast to the situation in our own lilliput democracy, the U.S.A. has not made a cult of mediocrity. And the ability to enthuse is still not suspect in the U.S.A., as it has been here for so long."

If one is to look around for a foreign author comparable to Elsa Gress, it must be the American Mary McCarthy, femme savante, critic, novelist and enfant terrible. And indeed, it is principally with American writers and theatre personalities Elsa Gress has established lifelong friendships and cooperation, and it is they who have enabled her to become a vehicle for inspiration derived from American drama.

A prolonged pause in the writing of fiction was only interrupted by the publication of *Habiba and Other Stories* (1964). Apart from this, Elsa Gress' publications have principally reflected her growing interest in the theatre, in addition to which there has been a deluge of essays, articles and comments on questions of topical interest. At frequent intervals they have been collected and published in book form, and as early as 1966 Hans Hertel made a comprehensive selection under the title of *The Professional Person*, in which the material was divided into categories according to theme. Since then, much more has been added, and so far Elsa Gress has 14 collections of articles of varying size to her name. They are all varied in content with the exception of *The Undiscovered Sex* from 1964, a well-structured, good-humoured and well-written book about prejudice and habitual thinking concerning the balance between man and woman. It stands as one of the most important contributions from that time to the debate on the position of women in society, but it is written entirely on Elsa Gress' own premises, and does not express the views of any individual movement. She and Women's Lib do not see eye to eye.

The Undiscovered Sex contains a warm foreword by Poul Henningsen, who describes Elsa Gress as "a resoundingly well-integrated troublemaker". They had a great respect for each other, and there are numerous points of similarity between these two enfants terribles, both of whom were so consistent in sustaining their own individualities that never for long were they associated with specific groups or opinions.

One newspaper editor has said of Elsa Gress that as a newspaper contributor she is unsurpassed at irritating one half of the readership and filling the other half with enthusiasm, though the same readers sometimes find themselves in one category, sometimes in the other.

In her articles and lectures she takes issue with doctrinaire marxism, extreme forms of feminism, and in general all kinds of one-sidedness. She looks for a golden mean, balance, breadth; she exhibits much of the seventeenth century's humanism and sense of the common good, but as a debater she often expresses herself aggressively and impatiently, which sometimes amuses and sometimes upsets her readers. In the heat of the moment she has expressed many unfair verdicts on those who think differently, verdicts given and sentences carried out without a chance of appeal. Somewhere or other, Jacob Paludan talks ironically of the tolerance which, as one becomes older, threatens one's best qualities. Elsa Gress has not been affected by this progressive weakening. On the contrary the effect she has on the discussion of current problems and attitudes is to set the adrenalin flowing more rapidly. Blows and insults are distributed generously – in principle in order to further tolerance, understanding and love among people and to spread enjoyment of and delight in the arts. It is a very civilised cause this militant debater is fighting for.

Some love mankind but cannot put up with individual human beings. Elsa Gress, however, fierce as she can be, has no wish to avoid people. She is really such a sociable person that she finds writing, with the solitude it entails, tedious. She feels a certain irritation as she goes over to the typewriter, where she writes as fast as she speaks in order to finish the job and get away to find company, preferably to pass on to others the thoughts she has just been committing to writing. This is particularly so if there is something which she and her friends can get together and organise as a joint project, propagating their ideas, making them catch fire and rise resplendent into full view.

This is one of the reasons why she is so interested in the theatre. Nor is she merely concerned to write the script and then leave it to the actors. No, what she seeks is teamwork in which all participate from start to finish, and text and music, dance, set design and action become one common undertaking, and play and work are fused into one. Together with her guests in Decenter, the centre of her artistic activities, she has devised and organised improvisations and happenings, some of which were once and for all affairs, while others were trial runs for shows that were to be given public performance. In her hefty volume of memoirs, *Compania* (1976) she describes the intensive interplay between herself and her friends and colleagues.

As a dramatist she has drawn her inspiration from fairground artists, medieval plays and the Renaissance theatre, but equally from her knowledge of modern American off Broadway drama, in particular the La Mama group, whose dynamic and successful leader, Tom O'Horgan, she has cooperated with for many years, and whose idea of total theatre transcending all boundaries has been one of her most powerful inspirations. Almost all her works for the stage were first written in English, and several were originally performed on the American student stage.

She sees her texts as musical scores, an incomplete part of the finished production, but they can make quite interesting reading, not least those in which she portrays historical figures in a philosophical and fictitious action. *Philoctetes Wounded* (produced on Danish television, directed by Tom O'Horgan) is about the artist Nicolai Abildgaard; *The Scapegoat or Donny Johnny* concerns Byron, who always provides good material for dramatic presentation. Together with other plays these two were published in *Demonic Ladies and Other Characters* (1979). Since then *Memory of the Future* and *The Feast of Ascension* have been performed on television and in the Gladsaxe Theatre respectively. Elsa Gress has been a kind of resident dramatist for the tiny experimental theatre called Riddersalen in Copenhagen, and her latest production there was *The Girl Who Trod on the Loaf* (1985).

The flamboyant world of the theatre is the setting for the novel *Salamander* (1977) with the demonic and fiery theatrical genius Roy Roscoe as its principal character, a director and composer on his brilliant path from the New York underground theatre to the established major theatres in the U.S.A. and Europe; he has an insatiable appetite for talent and human life, and is the flame that attracts the fluttering moths.

One of the moths attracted by him intellectually, artistically and erotically, is the Danish writer Lisa Bander – though she is not burned up by him. She experiences an ecstasy of art and love. She is married and has children; she has problems with her conscience, but she manages to avoid the breakdown of her marriage. Twenty years after *The Earth Is No Star* the reader is now presented with a new complicated relationship between a Dane and an American, but this time it is worked out with greater artistry and a more mature understanding of people, finely balanced between passion, sensitivity and a clear perspective, and with some lively close-ups of theatre personalities in Italy, London, New York, Copenhagen and Vienna.

This is Elsa Gress' most powerful novel so far. – If, that is to say, we are not to disregard the borderline between fiction and autobiography and then give the prize to the two volumes of memoirs, *My Many Homes* (1965) and *Free and Foreign* (1971). They contain and release something essential in her talent as an author and critic of her time, as a moralist and as a human being.

She has experienced more than most people, and in these books she demonstrates her outstanding ability to remember and to relive her experiences in such a way that they become vivid and real to her readers. This applies to the warm and burlesque account of her childhood and youth in a family environment which, to put it mildly, was unusual, totally dominated by the manic father figure. And it is equally true of the second volume, written in a different and more sombre tone, and portraying the world outside her childhood home, the world of nazism and war from the end of the thirties to the early postwar period. They show the author as a young and vulnerable woman in evil times, in her darkest hours feeling immersed in a well of loneliness and despair.

The original Danish title *Fuglefri og fremmed* is ambiguous. The word "fuglefri" implies "as free as a bird", but it also has a secondary meaning of "outlawed" – a person whose body hangs in the gallows, free for the birds to feed on.

In an interview Elsa Gress has said that there is no clear distinction between her novels and the memoirs as far as form and expression are concerned. But she adds that fiction has the advantage for the author that the characters portrayed can be given the fate they deserve.

Do she and her relatives, friends and colleagues in *My Many Homes* and *Free and Foreign* receive the fate they deserve? Perhaps after all there is one thing that gives good memoirs a different dimension from the made-up fantasies and fairytales of fiction. There is something particularly moving for the reader in seeing people of all kinds, happy and sad, foolish and wise, humble and self-assured, just as they were assigned their roles in the theatre of life and had to perform them to the bitter end, without an author to revise the script.

Elsa Gress is committed to her time, but she also acknowledges the obligation to accept the past. Her consciousness and understanding of history enable her to present herself as a pessimist in the short run but as an optimist in the long term.

Mogens Knudsen

133

Works by ELSA GRESS:

Strejftog. [Incursions]. [Essays]. Copenhagen: Hermann, 1945.

Mellemspil. [Interlude]. [Novel]. Copenhagen: Schultz, 1947.

Concertino. [Concertino]. [Novel]. Fredensborg: Arena, 1955.

Jorden er ingen stjerne. [The Earth Is No Star]. [Novel]. Fredensborg: Arena, 1956.

Nye strejftog. [Articles]. Fredensborg: Arena, 1957.

Elysisk Aften. – At være kætter. [Articles]. Fredensborg: Arena, 1959.

Prometheus på flugt. [Articles]. Fredensborg: Arena, 1961.

Er der nogen der hører efter? [Articles]. Fredensborg: Arena, 1964.

Habiba og andre noveller. [Habiba and Other Stories]. [Short sotries]. Copenhagen: Spectator, 1964.

Det uopdagede køn. [The Undiscovered Sex]. [Articles]. Copenhagen: Spectator, 1964.

Mine mange hjem. [My Many Homes]. [Memoirs]. Copenhagen: Spectator, 1965.

Det professionelle menneske. [The Professional Person]. [Articles]. Copenhagen: Gyldendal, 1966.

Om kløfter. [Articles]. Fredensborg: Arena, 1967.

Boxiganga. Teater som livsform. [Articles]. Copenhagen: Spectator, 1968.

Lurens toner. [Novel]. Copenhagen: Spectator, 1968.

Fugle og frøer. [Articles]. Fredensborg: Arena, 1969.

Den sårede Filoktet. (Philoctetes Wounded). [Play]. Gråsten: Forlaget Drama, 1970.*

Fuglefri og fremmed. [Free and Foreign]. [Memoirs]. Copenhagen: Gyldendal, 1971.

Apropos virkeligheden. [Articles]. Copenhagen: Gyldendal, 1972.

Compania 1-2. [Compania]. [Memoirs]. Copenhagen: Gyldendal, 1976.

Dramatikeren Soya. [Speech]. Copenhagen: Borgen, 1976.

Salamander. [Salamander]. [Novel]. Copenhagen: Gyldendal, 1977.

Engagement. [Articles]. Copenhagen: Gyldendal, 1977.

Dæmoniske damer og andre figurer. [Demonic Ladies and Other Characters]. [Plays]. Copenhagen: Gyldendal, 1979.

Fanden til forskel. [Articles]. Copenhagen: Gyldendal, 1979.

Vist koster det noget. [Memoirs]. Copenhagen: Berlingske, 1980.

Udsigter og indsigter. [Essays]. Brøndby Strand: Mistral, 1981.

Kristihimmelfartsfesten: et vulkanstykke. [The Feast of Ascension]. [Play]. Søborg: Nordiske Landes Forlag, 1983.

Blykuglen. [Essays]. Copenhagen: Gyldendal, 1984.

*Published in English:

Philoctetes Wounded and Other Plays. Glumsø: Decenter, 1969.

134

INGER CHRISTENSEN

and Other Women Poets

by *Uffe Harder*

Around 1950 the most popular woman poet in Denmark was without doubt Tove Ditlevsen (1918-1976), as she had been since the beginning of the 1940s. Her poetry is melodic, rhymed and often suitable for singing, and it deals with love, doubt, hope, loneliness and changing states of mind. It also often reflects her childhood background, the working class district of Vesterbro in Copenhagen. It is distinguished by a substantial psychological intuition and an unusually ruthless love of the truth which in later years, when she had dropped poetry in favour of prose, could result in merciless portraits of relationships between men and women living together.

She projected herself into what she wrote, and portrayed her own experiences in concrete and realistic detail. She became a myth while she was still alive, as indeed she still is. It can be argued that because of her special mixture of romanticism and realism she stands in the eyes of a large sector of the reading public as the last real, archetypal poet.

Already for several decades modernist poetry had been written in Denmark, though without ever assuming a dominant position. Examples can be named from the 1920s and 1930s such as Emil Bønnelykke and other late Expressionists, the cosmic-lyrical-erotic Jens August Schade who until long after the second world war practised his highly idiosyncratic Danish derivative of surrealism, and then the woman poet Bodil Bech (1889-1942), whose erotic and religious poems are imbued with an intensive vital sense.

After the upsurge of modernism in the 1950s, with its experimental use of imagery and freer associations, the 1960s saw the advent of concretism and then of systematised poetry to the accompaniment of political and ethical commitment. Documentary literature, known in Denmark as confessional literature, established itself firmly; in poetry it emerged in a form which was referred to as "chopped up prose" by one critic, because it was usually written in a somewhat pedestrian prose language with lines that were chopped up to resemble poetry. The important thing for these writers was definitely the message, the testimony, the things reported, and not the artistry.

One of them was Vita Andersen (b. 1944), who climbed into the public eye like a bright star. Her poems, for instance the collection called *Security Addicts*, tells of social and personal insecurity, a sense of isolation, and problems on the job. In one sense she appeared as a latter-day Tove Ditlevsen. Admittedly the form she adopted was different, but her poems were based on personal experiences, she was a person with whom readers could identify and in whose simple language they could recognise their own feelings and problems. And at the same time she was a fresh illustration of the myth about the girl from a modest background who makes a success of herself.

A poet of a completely different kind is Inger Christensen (b. 1935). Her poetry is not autobiographical, she lives a secluded life and does not court the public eye. There are many facets to her work, and in addition to poetry she writes novels, short prose pieces, essays and dramas, often experimental in nature. 25 years after Tove Ditlevsen she stood unchallenged as the most important and original woman poet in Denmark, a position which she has maintained ever since.

She started in 1962 with a volume entitled *Light*, which a year later was followed by one called *Grass*. The short titles are typical of one aspect of her work. Nature plays an important part in it, betokening growth and continuous development. The first poem in the first volume runs as follows:

If I stand
alone in the snow
it is clear
that I am a clock

how else would eternity
find its way around

Tr. by Susanna Nied

The speaker here is defined not through her personal story, but through her actions and statements. The language is simple, but the thought is in constant motion and can leap from one thing to another. For that reason it is always stimulating and inciting, and the reader is whisked along on a voyage of discovery that takes place instantaneously, as the poem is created.

In the most natural manner she makes use of what is at hand, and she takes liberties with it. She seems to feel at home in the natural world. A poem called "Peace" from *Grass* goes as follows:

Doves grow in the field
From dust thou shalt rise again

Tr. by Susanna Nied

Meanwhile, even in this volume there are also some long poems. And in 1964 and 1967 *Grass* was followed by the novels *The Eternity Machine* and *Azorno*.

Inger Christensen's major breakthrough came in 1969 with a volume of poems entitled *It*, a book of 238 pages, consisting of a Prologue and of three principal sections called "The Stage", "The Action" and "The Text", each again divided into subsections designated symmetries, transitivities, continuities, connexities, variabilities, extensions, integrities and universalities. It is a vast edifice, but its architecture is not static; it is rather a system of movements and changes, the directions of which are already indicated by the titles and subtitles. It is an attempt at a description of the world, an examination of forces, relationships and movements in it, in part a utopia and therefore implicitly a criticism of the established order.

It means that linguistic world that Inger Christensen is creating, a world whose limits writing is constantly seeking to transcend, and in this we probably find the most significant distinction between her and her Danish predecessors. The following is the sixth poem in "Stage/symmetries".

Everything is put in place and taken away:

oceans are filled in with countries
rivers are filled in with roads
lakes are filled in with islands

141

extra ice masses,
hidden springs and groundwater,
water in sewers, oases,
raindrops, dew, all are gathered
poured into volcanoes, evaporate;

abysses are filled in with mountains,
subways with houses,
houses with still more houses,
cities with cities, all with all,
till everything is full,
till everything is whole, without division,
impossible to divide,
and with no correlates in language.

Everything can thereupon and therefore be taken away
and put in some completely different place.

Tr. by Susanna Nied

She works with systems. The principle in *It* is reminiscent of that in grammar, and she has probably derived a good deal of inspiration from modern French linguistic philosophy. She organises her world as grammar organises language, but within each category there is great freedom of movement, and in this particular case it is she herself who is creating the rules, establishing categories and deciding within which categories the individual phenomena and activities are to be placed. This she does on the basis of her theoretical knowledge and in consequence of her analytical, critical activities, but it also stems from her sensitivity, her direct experience, her feeling and her imagination. The text is the result of the poet's play with these elements; it loses its innocence because choices are made during the writing process, but it does not therefore necessarily lose its originality.

A special feature of Inger Christensen's poetry is its musicality. Anyone who has heard her read her own early poems will know that she almost sang them, and this particular manner of reciting them is not only due to the soft, singing East Jutlandic intonation which is part of her, but it presumably also resulted from her surrendering herself to the message of the poems; in addition it helped build up her concentration so that she could always be completely unaffected by the surroundings in which she chanced to find herself.

Musicality implies being in harmony with something, and this is also an aspect of Inger Christensen's work which it is important to observe. This musicality is spontaneous and is achieved spontaneously, as emerges from the special sound and atmosphere of her sentences. The reader senses a strange, almost somnambulistic familiarity with elemental, fundamental, immanent phenomena, whether they be great or small. The quotations from her early poetry illustrate this clearly. Meanwhile, examples of this can also be found in her prose works, not least in the story "The Painted Room" (1976), inspired in part by paintings by the baroque artist Mantegna, but also by her views on power games, for Inger Christensen is rarely totally non-political. They are also to be found in the charming little *April Letter* (1979), based on a spring visit to Paris in the company of a very young son and his boundless and spontaneous hunger and ability to experience balanced against the reactions and attitudes evinced by his knowing mother.

Her most recent volume of poems, *Alphabet* (1981) opens like a fan. The first poem in it consists of one single line ("apricot trees exist, apricot trees exist"), and the fourteenth and last, which begins with the letter n and in reality consists of several poems, is made up of a large number of lines indeed. Just how many can presumably be worked out by any computer fed with the information that in Fibonacci's sequence of numbers, which decides the lengths of the individual sections here, every new term after and including 3 is the sum of the two preceding. So here, too, there is a system, this time a mathematical one. The form is based on it, but at the same time the poet nevertheless goes her own way: the last sections up to and including the one beginning with the letter n consist of several different poems which, apart from the first, can begin with any letter. They have no theme in common apart from the all-embracing one of the multiplicity of the world and the delight it inspires, our responsibility for it and the fear that it could be grossly and rapidly diminished. The system seems to be fundamental to the work, just like composition in a piece of music. It arranges the material but not the content or the tone of the poems, and the development of the various sections emphasises multiplicity, which is the principal theme. But this development is then interrupted at an arbitrarily chosen point, a little more than half way through the alphabet. That, too, could be interpreted in various ways.

Alphabet is perhaps the most beautiful book Inger Christensen has written so far. It contains a glorious array of plants, minerals, animals, birds, fruits, colours and associations, perfumes and perspectives which must fill every reader with a sense of happiness, but there is also a carefully controlled expression of fear, cold, icy and total, all the more powerful as the sounds and changing rhythms from poem to poem in fact give the text something of the quality of music. For instance music like this:

it's new for me
       to be hearing cicadas
              here where it's cold
                     and so there are none

perhaps it's the kind
       of thing that's always happened
              when the light travels north
                     and the birches go along

as when a room from
       a dream on a trip
              is the same room that you
                     come home and move into

there's a drawing of
       an encapsuled child
              crouched in a crystal
                     that's not especially big

as if in dreams
        dreamed not by people
                animals or birds
                        but by insects perhaps

perhaps by the traveler
        himself who is looking
                away from himself for a while
                        and is spread in the birches' haze

perhaps by a child who persistently
        examines a lake in the forest
                and finds that the soul might well
                        have been dreamed by cicadas

it sometimes happens
        when the snow melts
                that all it has hidden
                        comes out so the soul can be seen

as when death doesn't really
        become visible until
                somebody looks at the gift
                        that the dead person took to the
                                                    grave

I think it must look like
        the tarnished metal box
                I've known for a long time
                        I'm carrying with me

it doesn't contain
        any more than a coin
                a tooth, a silver thimble
                        and a little empty bottle

but its scent when
        it's opened
                fills everything
                        like midnight sun

this is how I've imagined
        being able to imagine:
                a space of clear crystal
                        around the deathbed

where the dead person first
        really looks like himself
                        by dying away from the others

Tr. by Susanna Nied

In 1982, the year after the appearance of *Alphabet*, Inger Christensen published a collection of essays called *Part of the Labyrinth*, which gives an excellent brief impression of both the manner and the content of her thinking. In a piece on Dante – which, moreover, she starts by arguing that one of the reasons for reading him is that he is unreadable – she writes that "structure and systematism, art and philosophy work their way through a wickerwork of different currents moving towards unity – unity which at the end of the artistic process must be returned to its starting point – the world, which is unreadable in principle." She ends the same essay by remarking that: "Dante was, of course, not synonymous with his work. He was at once the principal character and the person who set the action in motion. One could almost say his work is a political act in which he applies his theories and experiences until the vision of the new world, the new life, takes shape before his eyes. He knew it beforehand, but wrote it in order to get to know it. And wrote it to make the world readable up to the point or moment when the author and the world must coincide in their common unreadableness." One could scarcely imagine a better description of the practice followed by Inger Christensen in her own poetry.

In *Part of the Labyrinth* she also demonstrates a certain predi-

146

lection for the baroque. In one place she describes it as a "struggle to decide between the rights of gods and men to the conceit"; and the conceit must not least imply creating and activating models and systems. But: "Who has invented whom, and who can contemplate whom?" The world is unreadable, and in order to make it readable we have to write our own interpretation into it, and this is precisely what she does.

She quotes Descartes' "I think, therefore I am" and suggests that he could have written: "I think, and therefore I am a part of the labyrinth", and she goes on: "The labyrinth is like a sort of common approach, a Möbius strip between men and the world – and in that kind of labyrinth it is really only children who can feel at home; for they break the spell by turning the magic into reality." And this, of course, is exactly what can be learned from *April Letter.* In a text entitled "5 × 25 Wintry Projects for a Summer Project", still in *Part of the Labyrinth,* Inger Christensen says, doubtless with a reference to Claude Lévi-Strauss's *La pensée sauvage:* "Nature – what is untamed – untamed thought is beyond good and evil. Man has overcome the untamed instead of overcoming evil. That is why we have lost our independence."

The labyrinth as a Möbius strip – i.e. a strip which turns first one side forward, then the other – between mankind and the world. What world? Clearly not the world created by men, and therefore it must be the one created by nature. To which one should perhaps add those elements in it which *were* created by human beings in an earlier age. And independence in relation to what? Presumably in relation to doctrines, in relation to what has already been created, already thought. Inger Christensen says that mankind has overcome the untamed, that is to say those things which determine the extent of our choice, and from which a renewal can come; yet nevertheless, this is what she still defends as though, even if overcome, it is not totally destroyed. Probably it is also that which determines the unusually organic character of all her writing, and the apparently effortless radicalism with which it is imbued.

One final aspect of Inger Christensen's work, to which few

references are made, is her humour. It is expressed gently and quietly, a kind of cool merriment with quite far-reaching implications.

In the same year as *It* was published, 1969, Kirsten Thorup (b. 1942) published her poems called *Love from Trieste*, which was followed in 1971 by *It's Daisy Today*. Like *It*, they are a clear indication that something new has taken place in Danish women's poetry. The language has been relativised; it is no longer the writer speaking directly, but models and fictitious characters she has set in motion. They represent the forces and attitudes and sensitivities of her own generation and the succeeding one. The texts are glossy and cosmopolitan and characterised by a pseudo-innocent, nihilistic imagination which can at times also be cruel. They can be read as a punk-like *Beggar's Opera* from a time before punk emerged and perhaps as a report on society in which poetry has got the upper hand.

Like Kirsten Thorup, Dorrit Willumsen (b. 1940) has mainly written prose, but a number of poems in a book of poems and short stories called *Coppelia the Model* (1973) and in the collection of poems entitled *Contacts* (1976) nevertheless occupy a significant place in the poetry of women writers in the years with which we are concerned. They are about life in a technologically advanced, almost science fiction consumer society in which the inhabitants find it difficult to live up to their roles as models, mannequins and faultlessly functioning robots. Dorrit Willumsen has a keen sense of the burlesque and grotesque; her poetical style contains echoes of surrealism; and behind it all one senses an element of desperation kept strictly under control:

Coffee with Whisky and Cream

She sees
how the whisky
blends with the coffee
how dark sugar
sinks
deep down in the glass

how the cream
nestles close to the side
affectionate white
and light

She drinks
and feels
the heat
increasing
her depression
sinking
deep down
And no spoon
in sudden movement
makes these dark granules
rise
With cautious lips
she slowly
sips
gently enjoying
till all is
like white light whipped
cream

The beginning of the 1980s apparently coincided with a return to
a more personal, individual way of writing. Among the women
poets who have already distinguished themselves is Pia Tafdrup
(b. 1952), whose first poems are given the title *When an Angel's
Been Grazed*:

Sweeps the dead birds
down from the kitchen shelf
and washes her hands

of the damp disquiet
that leaves its traces everywhere
on doors and ledges

falls
and knocks her knees and hands and nose
on the floor in the empty house

and knows the smell
when an angel's been grazed

This volume contains poems about childhood and about feeling
death in your immediate vicinity, but in particular it contains a
number of erotic poems, poems about wanting and wanting to be
wanted, about bodies together or longing to be together. Or
rather, these various experiences and states are fused into each
other. The images – snails, leaves, earth – are taken from
nature, but the poems emerge and take shape in what Pia Tafdrup
in the title of her latest book calls *The Innermost Zone* (1983).
Her language is sensuous, assured and varied, vibrant with life
right out to the furthest ramifications of the sentences. In this
"inner zone" you can experience how "this evening a heart is
taking wing/ to alight on a radiant chestnut tree", and in the
morning you can "see dead dream cells/ spread/ in sudden white
light".

Another woman poet who has attracted attention is Juliane
Preisler (b. 1959) with her two volumes *Without* (1983) and *Into*
(1984). Her poems seem at the same time to be both taut and
effervescent. Taut because the pregnant words and juxtapositions
come at such brief intervals, and effervescent because they often
seem to go in different directions and because the links between
them, like the syntax on many occasions, are broken, resulting in
individual sections detaching themselves from the overall framework that the reader was about to establish. But then, who has
asked the reader to establish any definitive cohesion, or the poet
to postulate one?

All one can do is to draw around Juliane Preisler's poems a
circle big enough to contain all the movements within them, all
the leaps, all the points of reference and all the elements giving
meaning, and then to reread them. They are often very beautiful
and both the individual sequences and the points of contact be-

tween them can be laden with intensity. Taken individually, they are compact, as though the poet has wanted to write them using the smallest possible number of choice words. The following is an example from *Without*:

They have given me
but
I am stung
All the gifts
were smiling
and now they cry out

For terrible was
the journey
towards birth
of sharp little
children
who crept
forward
in the night
and tore
with their claws

Juliane Preisler obviously does not tell stories. The stuff on which she bases her poems is perhaps not even always related to the same time, but to concrete experiences – of childhood, of the transition from one phase to another, of the relationships between people and of the interaction of her inner and outer worlds, an interaction occasionally marked by conflict. The dynamism in her poems and in the universe she creates in order, in the words of Inger Christensen, to make it readable, depends on its seeming to be in a constant process of coming into being and at the same time disappearing. It is this movement, into consciousness and into oblivion, that is expressed in the disjointed, pointilliste style. As well as the moments when a sufficient number of elements assert themselves on the reader's consciousness at the same time.

The poetry written by women during these years is, like all the poetry written in Denmark at that time, rich in invention and expressive of a high degree of linguistic awareness. Among the young poets who ought also to be mentioned in this brief survey is Merete Torp (b. 1956) who published her first volume, entitled *Poems* in 1982. In contrast to Juliane Preisler's they constitute a long, coherent sequence of mainly short poems in which the writer, faced with the dark and her sense of the vast extent and age of the universe, before which everything assumes the same insignificance, seeks to formulate a personal way of coping with life.

Celestial Bodies

The foam the froth
we see
our eyes half
closed
in rest

We are raised by the heat
we shall be lifted, are lifted
by this bursting calm

We need no deathly gravity
no contourless shield
we are bound to a substance
a powder of globes

We had to leave a form
behind, with a painful grasp
it lacked every blinding dawn

There were dull colors and glowing
none as glowing
as the form
we laid
waste
Tr. by Poul Borum

Uffe Harder

Works by INGER CHRISTENSEN:

Lys. [Light]. [Poems]. Copenhagen: Gyldendal, 1962.*
Græs. [Grass]. [Poems]. Copenhagen: Gyldendal, 1963.*
Evighedsmaskinen. [The Eternity Machine]. [Novel]. Copenhagen: Gyldendal, 1964.
Azorno. [Azorno]. [Novel]. Copenhagen: Gyldendal, 1967.
Det. [It]. [Poems]. Copenhagen: Gyldendal, 1969.*
Intriganterne. [Play]. Copenhagen: Gyldendal, 1972.
Det malede værelse. [Novel]. Copenhagen: Brøndum, 1976.
Brev i april. [April letter]. [Poems]. Copenhagen: Brøndum, 1979.
Alfabet. [Alphabet]. [Poems]. Copenhagen: Gyldendal, 1981.
Del af labyrinten. [Part of the Labyrinth]. [Essays]. Copenhagen: Gyldendal, 1982.
Den store ukendte rejse. [Textbook]. Copenhagen: Gad, 1982.

*Published in English:

Selection of poems from the collections *Lys* and *Græs* published in different anthologies. For further reference see: *A Bibliography of Danish Literature 1950-1980.* Copenhagen: Det danske Selskab, 1982.
A complete but as yet unpublished translation of *Det* by Susanna Nied.

Works by PIA TAFDRUP:

Når der går hul på en engel. [When an Angel's been Grazed]. [Poems]. Copenhagen: Borgen, 1981.
Konstellationer – en antologi af dansk lyrik. [Anthology]. Herning: Systime, 1982.
Intetfang. [Poems]. Copenhagen: Borgen, 1982.
Den inderste zone. [The Innermost Zone]. [Poems]. Copenhagen: Borgen, 1983.
Springflod. [Poems]. Copenhagen: Borgen, 1985.

Works by JULIANE PREISLER:

Uden. [Without]. [Poems]. Copenhagen: Borgen, 1983.
Ind. [Into]. [Poems]. Copenhagen: Borgen, 1984.
Standset aften. [Novels]. Copenhagen: Borgen, 1985.

Works by MERETE TORP:

Digte. [Poems]. Copenhagen: Gyldendal, 1982.

153

PIA TAFDRUP (b. 1952) has travelled throughout Scandinavia where she has had poetry readings in Norway and Finland. She has contributed poems to several anthologies and articles to various periodicals and newspapers.

JULIANE PREISLER (b. 1959) reviews for the newspaper *Information*. She has made a name as a poet with poems in the periodical *Hvedekorn* and in the Poetry Year Book 1983, followed by two published collections of poems.

MERETE TORP (b. 1956) has contributed poems to *Hvedekorn* and other literary periodicals. In her poems observation/abstraction/comparison are concentrated in one vertiginous unity.

THE AUTHORS

MARIANNE JUHL, literary critic. Born 1943. M.A. in Danish and film 1971. Taught at Kolding Grammar School 1971-73. Reviews television and literature on the Copenhagen newspaper *Berlingske Tidende*.

Marianne Juhl has made a special study of Karen Blixen. In 1981 she published a book entitled *Diana's Revenge*, seeking to get behind the mask of Karen Blixen's work. Basing herself on Blixen's *Letters from Africa* and certain stories, she draws a picture of a modern woman's breach with nineteenth century views of life and her struggle to discover her own identity.

THORKILD BJØRNVIG, author. Born 1918. M.A. in comparative literature at Århus University 1947. Dr. phil. Århus 1964. Member of The Danish Academy. His profound knowledge of literature, philosophy and culture is the basis of his own work as a writer. Both in his own poems and essays and in his research and translations of foreign poetry Bjørnvig has sought to resolve the essential problem of his relationship to the surrounding world.

For many years Thorkild Bjørnvig was closely associated with Karen Blixen. This friendship inspired his poem "The Childhood House" and his book *The Pact*, which centres on the question of "Who am I?" Bjørnvig and Blixen disagreed in principle on the answer. The result was a struggle "about where in the final analysis we should establish our identity and discover who we were: whether it was a historical or a cosmic problem".

AAGE HENRIKSEN, professor. Born 1921. M.A. in Scandinavian literature from Copenhagen University 1947. Lecturer in Danish at Lund University 1949-55. Dr. phil. 1954. Attached to Radio Denmark 1955-61. Subsequently lecturer/assistant professor and reader/associate professor and since 1968 Professor of Scandinavian Literature at Copenhagen University.

Aage Henriksen knew Karen Blixen well, and all his work on her has to be seen against the background of an inspiring and problematical relationship to her.

Aage Henriksen has occupied an important position in Danish literary research. His constant efforts to relate the experience of everyday life to the development of humanist theory has in recent years brought him into fields such as the sociology of knowledge and philosophical hermeneutics.

TORBEN BROSTRØM, professor and author. Born 1927. M.A. in Danish and French at Copenhagen University 1953. Attached to the newspaper *Information* as literary critic, also concerned with works of criticism and literary theory. Professor of Danish Literature at the Royal Danish School of Educational Studies since 1979. Editor and co-editor of several Danish periodicals, *Hvedekorn* 1955-60, *Vindrosen* 1965-68 and *Selvsyn* 1960-66. Member of The Danish Academy.

As a critic Torben Brostrøm pioneered the English and American school of new criticism in Scandinavia, and he has applied this analytical method to a large number of difficult works of literature, thereby making them more easily accessible and relevant.

JENS KISTRUP, critic. Born 1925. M.A. in Danish literature from Copenhagen University 1949. In 1946 he became film critic for the newspaper *Berlingske Tidende*, and is now that paper's drama and literature critic.

Jens Kistrup is a skilful promoter of modern literature. In what he calls an "age of confusion" he believes that the essential task for a critic is to distinguish the various shades of opinion in the general discussion of the multifariousness of truth; he must then compare and contrast them in order to put conflicting views within the fields of drama, literature and public debate into perspective without resorting to ideological simplification.

Jens Kistrup's principle as a critic is "to recommend and whet the appetite rather than to sit in judgement and give marks".

BODIL WAMBERG, lecturer. Born 1929. M.A. in Danish and English from Copenhagen University. Lecturer at the Royal Danish School of Educational Studies since 1970.

Bodil Wamberg has written articles in newspapers and periodicals and also made a number of broadcasts. She has written several books, including a study of the author Leif Panduro entitled *Crazy Love* (1978) and one of the authoress Agnes Henningsen called *The Price of Improvidence* (1983). In addition Bodil Wamberg contributed to the history of Danish literature in the twentieth century, (*Danske digtere i det tyvende århundrede*) (1982), and is at present working on a book about the actress and authoress Johanne Luise Heiberg (1812-90).

ERIK VAGN JENSEN, publisher. Born 1930. B.Sc. (Econ.) 1958. Folk High School teacher 1958-62. Publishing editor with *Gyldendal*, Denmark's largest publishing house, 1962-79. Managing Director of the *Vindrose* publishing house since 1980. Vindrose is closely associated with the American Curbstone Press (Willimantic) in connection with the publication of Danish literature in the USA.

Erik Vagn Jensen has written articles in periodicals and newspapers. He also contributed to the history of Danish literature in the twentieth century (*Danske digtere i det tyvende århundrede*) (1982) with an article on the writer Angelo Hjort.

MOGENS KNUDSEN, publisher. Born 1919. M.A. in comparative literature at Copenhagen University 1943. Attached to *Gyldendal* 1945-51, and to Radio Denmark 1951-61. Publishing editor at Gyldendal 1961 and since 1964 Director, responsible for Danish literature and in charge of relations with authors.

Over the years Mogens Knudsen has maintained not only quality but also

158

continuity, breadth and comprehensiveness in the production of this large publishing house. He has at the same time been active as a translator and author. In his writing he works with subjects on the borderline between literary and cultural history.

UFFE HARDER, author. Born 1930. M.A. in French and English at Copenhagen University 1957. Employed in the literature section of Radio Denmark 1961-73. Critic on the newspaper *Information*, editor of Danish and foreign journals. Member of The Danish Academy.

Both in a private capacity and as a writer, Uffe Harder has built up a network of contacts at home and abroad. Thanks to his linguistic talent he has acted as a link between Danish and foreign literature. In his attempt to demonstrate points of contact between cultures near and far he has, for instance, translated and re-created French-language poetry from Africa. At the same time much of his own work has been translated into other languages.

SELECT BIBLIOGRAPHY

Note: The vowels æ, ø and å follow z in the Danish alphabet and are alphabetized accordingly.

The bibliography does not pretend to be exhaustive. It consists of a selection from the works of Danish women writers and poets after 1960. Only for writers mentioned in this book is reference made to works from before this date.

In general only complete works are listed, though as far as practicable such parts of works as are available in English translation have been included.

Authors are listed alphabetically, then works chronologically. The date of first publication is given, even when the works of certain authors (especially Karen Blixen and Tove Ditlevsen) have appeared in later editions.

An English title in square brackets after the original Danish indicates that the title has been translated thus in the main text, but that the work is only available in Danish. An asterisk, however, means that the work has been published in English, either in full or in part, and bibliographical information on such translations is then added at the end of each individual entry. It has not always been possible to trace the original Danish titles of isolated extracts.

AGGER, RAGNHILD (b. 1918)

Pladser. [Novel]. Copenhagen: Gyldendal, 1973.
På grænsen. [Short stories]. Copenhagen: Lindhardt & Ringhof, 1982.
Tågelandet. [Novel]. Lindhardt & Ringhof, 1985.

ANDERSEN, VITA (b. 1944)

Tryghedsnarkomaner. [Security Addicts]. [Poems]. Copenhagen: Gyldendal, 1977.*
Næste kærlighed eller Laila og de andre. [Poems]. Copenhagen: Brøndum, 1978.
Hold kæft og vær smuk: 12 noveller. [Short stories]. Copenhagen: Gyldendal, 1978.

*Published in English:

Selection of poems from this collection. Tr. Jannick Storm and Linda Lappin. In: *Modern Poetry in Translation*, No. 33. N.Y. 1978.

ARNBAK, BIRTHE (b. 1923)

Morgenstund: billeder fra en barndom. [Poems]. Copenhagen: Gyldendal, 1975.
Jeg ser dig allevegne. [Poems]. Copenhagen: Gyldendal, 1977.*
Min engelske sommer. [Novel]. Copenhagen: Lindhardt & Ringhof, 1981.
Hans og Grete: seks noveller. [Short stories]. Copenhagen: Lindhardt & Ringhof, 1984.
Forventningens land. [Poems]. Copenhagen: Gyldendal, 1985.

*Published in English:

Selection of poems from this collection. Tr. Anne Born. In: *Orbis* No. 35. Derbeyshire: International Poetry Society, 1979.

BAIDEL, LOLA (b. 1951)

Du skal passe din have. [Poems]. Copenhagen: Klitrose, 1979.*
Små hop på stedet. [Novel]. Copenhagen: Klitrose, 1983.
Døren er åben. [Poems]. Copenhagen: Klitrose, 1984.

*Published in English:

Selected poems from this and other collections: *The Mistress of Laughter.* Tr. Mark Hebsgaard. Copenhagen: Klitrose, 1983.

BECH, BODIL (1889-1942)

Vi der ejer natten. [Poems]. Copenhagen: Gyldendal, 1934.
Ildtunger danser. [Poems]. Copenhagen: Gyldendal, 1935.
Granit og dugg. [Poems]. Copenhagen: Jespersen & Pio, 1938.*
Ud af himmelporte. [Poems]. Copenhagen: Martin, 1941.

*Published in English:

In the Train. Poem from this collection. Tr. Charles Wharton Stork, 1947. In: *A Second Book of Danish Verse.* Rpt. Freeport, N.Y.: Books for Library Press, 1968.

BLIXEN, KAREN, see p. 56-57

BORBERG, JYTTE (b. 1917)

Eline Bessers læretid. [Novel]. Copenhagen: Gyldendal, 1976.
Det bedste og det værste: Eline Besser til det sidste. [Novel]. Copenhagen: Gyldendal, 1977.
Nu og aldrig. [Novel]. Copenhagen: Gyldendal, 1979.
Sjælen er gul. [Novel]. Copenhagen: Tiderne Skifter, 1981.
Slaraffenland. [Novel]. Charlottenlund: Rosinante, 1982.
Skyggernes bog. [Novel]. Charlottenlund: Rosinante, 1983.

BRØGGER, SUZANNE, see p. 88

BUHL, INGEBORG (1890-1982)

Vjera og andre fortællinger. [Short stories]. Copenhagen: Borgen, 1961.
Ad veje du ikke ved. [Short stories]. Copenhagen: Hasselbach, 1964.
Skyggeliv: maskebal på hjemmet. [Novel]. Herning: Poul Kristensen, 1977.

BØDKER, CECIL (b. 1927)

Øjet. [Short stories]. Fredensborg: Arena, 1961.
Samlede digte. [Poems]. Copenhagen: Hasselbach, 1964.
Tilstanden Harley. [Novel]. Fredensborg: Arena, 1965.
I vædderens tegn. [Poems]. Copenhagen: Arena, 1968.
Silas. [Juvenile literature, series]. Different Danish publishers, 1969-.*
Salthandlerskens hus. [Travel book]. Copenhagen: Arena, 1972.
En vrangmaske i Vorherres strikketøj. [Novel]. Copenhagen: Arena, 1974.
Evas ekko. [Novel]. Viborg: Arena, 1980.
Tænk på Jolande. [Novel]. Viborg: Arena, 1981.

*Published in English:

Several *Silas* books: *Silas and Ben-Godik* (1978). *Silas and the Black Mare* (1980). *Silas and the Runaway* (1978). N.Y.: Delacorte Press.

CEDERSTRAND, DITTE (1915-1984)

De uspurgtes historie. [Continued novel]. Copenhagen: Vinten, 1975-.
Revolutionens ørn: 13 billeder af Rosa Luxemburgs liv. [Play]. Copenhagen: Medusa, 1979.

CHRISTENSEN, INGER, see p. 153

CHRISTENSEN, MARTHA (b. 1926)

Vær god ved Remond. [Novel]. Copenhagen: Fremad, 1962.
I den skarpe middagssol. [Novel]. Copenhagen: Fremad, 1972.
Som de vil ha' dig. [Novel]. Copenhagen: Fremad, 1974.
Vores egen Irene. [Novel]. Copenhagen: Fremad, 1976.
En fridag til fru Larsen. [Novel]. Copenhagen: Fremad, 1977.
Borgmesteren sover. [Novel]. Copenhagen: Fremad, 1979.
I gårs fortræd. [Novel]. Copenhagen: Fremad, 1981.
Hvis vi elskede mere. [Short stories]. Copenhagen: Fremad, 1982.
Tusindfryd. [Novel]. Copenhagen: Fremad, 1984.

CLOD, BENTE (b. 1946)

Brud: portræt af en udvikling. [Novel]. Copenhagen: Gyldendal, 1977.
Syv sind. [Novel]. Copenhagen: Gyldendal, 1980.
Vent til du hører mig le. [Novel]. Copenhagen: Gyldendal, 1983.

DAHLERUP, ULLA (b. 1942)

Gløder i asken. [Novel]. Copenhagen: Hirschsprung, 1961.
Søstrene. [Novel]. Copenhagen: Gyldendal, 1979.

DINESEN, ISAK, see Blixen, Karen.

DITLEVSEN, TOVE (1917-1976)

Pigesind. [Poems]. Copenhagen: Rasmus Naver, 1939.*
Den fulde frihed. [Complete Freedom and Other Stories]. [Short stories]. Copen-
    hagen: Athenæum, 1944.*
Blinkende lygter. [The Blinking Lights]. [Poems]. Copenhagen: Athenæum,
    1947.*
To som elsker hinanden. [Novel]. Copenhagen: Hasselbach, 1960.
Den hemmelige rude. [Poems]. Copenhagen: Hasselbach, 1961.*
Den onde lykke. [Short stories]. Copenhagen: Hasselbach, 1963.*
Barndom. [Childhood]. [Memoirs]. Copenhagen: Hasselbach, 1967.*
Ungdom. [Youth]. [Memoirs]. Copenhagen: Hasselbach, 1967.*

Ansigterne. [Novel]. Copenhagen: Hasselbach, 1968.*
De voksne. [Poems]. Copenhagen: Gyldendal, 1969.*
Det runde værelse. [Poems]. Copenhagen: Gyldendal, 1973.*
Vilhelms værelse. [Novel]. Copenhagen: Gyldendal, 1975.
Til en lille pige: efterladte digte. [Poems]. Copenhagen: Gyldendal, 1978.

*Published in English:

Selection of poems from Tove Ditlevsen's collections are published in different anthologies. For further reference see: *A Bibliography of Danish Literature,* Copenhagen: Det danske Selskab, 1982.
Complete Freedom and Other Stories. Tr. Jack Brøndum. Willimantic, Conn. CT: Curbstone Press, 1982.
Early Spring. [Childhood & Youth]. Tr. Tiina Nunnally. Washington, Seattle WA: The Seal Press, 1985.

DREWSEN, JETTE (b. 1943)

Hvad tænkte egentlig Arendse? [Novel]. Copenhagen: Gyldendal, 1972.
Fuglen. [Novel]. Copenhagen: Gyldendal, 1974.
Tid og sted. [Novel]. Copenhagen: Gyldendal, 1978.
Midtvejsfester. [Novel]. Copenhagen: Gyldendal, 1980.
Ingen erindring. [Novel]. Copenhagen: Gyldendal, 1983.

ENEVOLD, KAREN (b. 1896)

Den femte dag. [Short stories]. Copenhagen: Gyldendal, 1975.
Det leende. [Novel]. Copenhagen: Gyldendal, 1979.
Kongens nar. [Short stories]. Copenhagen: Gyldendal, 1980.

ERIKSEN, INGE (b. 1935)

Victoria og verdensrevolutionen. [Novel]. Copenhagen: Gyldendal, 1976.
Vinden er ikke til salg. [Play]. Copenhagen: Klitrose, 1980.
Silkehavet: en sørøverroman. [Novel]. Copenhagen: Klitrose, 1981.
Amanda Screamers begær: en føljetonroman. [Novel]. Copenhagen: Klitrose, 1982.
Luderen fra Gomorra. [Novel]. Copenhagen: Rhodos, 1983.
Fuga for en stum nomade. [Novel]. Copenhagen: Gyldendal, 1984.
Nord for tiden. [Novel]. Copenhagen: Gyldendal, 1985.

GIACOBBE, MARIA (b. 1928)

Lærerinde på Sardinien. [Novel]. Copenhagen: Aschehoug, 1961.
Havet. [Novel]. Copenhagen: Gyldendal, 1967.
Eurydike. [Novel]. Copenhagen: Gyldendal, 1970.
Dagbog mellem to verdener. [Memoirs]. Copenhagen: Gyldendal, 1975.
De frie læretider. [Poems]. Copenhagen: Gyldendal, 1981.
Den blinde fra Smyrna. [Short stories]. Copenhagen: Gyldendal, 1982.
Den dag vi vågner. [Essays]. Copenhagen: Gyldendal, 1983.

GIESE, SUZANNE (b. 1946)

På andre tanker. [Novel]. Copenhagen: Tiderne Skifter, 1978.
Brændende kærlighed. [Novel]. Copenhagen: Vindrose, 1984.

GRESS, ELSA, see p. 134

GRØNFELDT, VIBEKE (b. 1948)

Djævlens trekant. [Novels: Erika. Josef. Penelope]. Tidsvilde: Charlatan, 1975.
Den første sne. [Novel]. Copenhagen: Gyldendal, 1979.
Baglandet. [Short stories]. Copenhagen: Vindrose, 1981.
Det fantastiske barn. [Novel]. Copenhagen: Gyldendal, 1982.
Tidens tilbud. [Novel]. Copenhagen: Gyldendal, 1983.
Den blanke sol. [Novel]. Copenhagen: Gyldendal, 1985.

HANSEN, AASE (1893-1981)

Luftspejling over havet. [Novel]. Copenhagen: Spektrum, 1963.
Nogle dage, nogle timer. [Novel]. Copenhagen: Spektrum, 1966.
Gæster i december. [Novel]. Copenhagen: Wøldike, 1970.
I Forvitringens Aar. [Novel]. Copenhagen: Wøldike, 1977.

HEMMER HANSEN, EVA (1913-1983)

Skandale i Troja. [Novel]. Copenhagen: Fremad, 1954.*
Camelot: en roman om mænd. [Novel]. Copenhagen: Fremad, 1966.

*Published in English:

Scandal in Troy. Tr. Dorothy F. Grimm & Sven O. Karell. N.Y.: Popular Library, 1957.

JEINER, NANNA (b. 1942)

Afrodite tar hjem og andre digte om kærlighed. [Poems]. Copenhagen: Gylden-
    dal, 1978.
Mellem fire vægge: 40 digte. [Poems]. Copenhagen: Gyldendal, 1979.

JENSEN, HANNE MARIE (b. 1949)

Tilbagetoget. [Poems]. Copenhagen: Gyldendal, 1979.

JENSEN, GRETE STENBÆK, see Stenbæk Jensen, Grete

LARSEN, MARIANNE (b. 1951)

Koncentrationer. [Poems]. Copenhagen: Borgen, 1971.
Overstregslyd. [Poems]. Copenhagen: Borgen, 1972.*
21 digte. [Poems]. Copenhagen: Jorinde & Joringel, 1972.
Modsætninger. [Poems]. Copenhagen: Borgen, 1975.
Handlinger. [Poems]. Copenhagen: Borgen, 1976.
Hvem er fjenden?: klassepoesi. [Poems]. Copenhagen: Borgen, 1977.
Opgørelse følger. [Poems]. Copenhagen: Borgen, 1978.
Det kunne være nu. [Poems]. Copenhagen: Borgen, 1979.
Hinandens kræfter. [Poems]. Copenhagen: Borgen, 1980.
Der er et håb i mit hoved. [Poems]. Copenhagen: Borgen, 1981.
Bag om maskerne. [Poems]. Copenhagen: Borgen, 1982.
Udvalgte digte 1969-82. [Poems]. Copenhagen: Borgen, 1983.
Kære levende. [Poems]. Copenhagen: Borgen, 1983.
Direkte. [Poems]. Copenhagen: Borgen, 1984.
Pludselig dette. [Poems]. Copenhagen: Borgen, 1985.

*Published in English:

Selected poems from this and other collections in: Contemporary Danish Poetry.
    Boston: Twayne Publishers, 1977.
Selected Poems. Tr. Nadia Christensen. Willimantic, CT: Augustinus/Curbsto-
    ne, 1982.

LIVBJERG, BIRGITTE (b. 1940)

Kærligheden findes. [Poems]. Copenhagen: Gyldendal, 1978.
Hovedet over kroppen: egoist digte. [Poems]. Copenhagen: Gyldendal, 1979.
Døtre og elskerinder. [Novel]. Copenhagen: Fremad, 1983.
Søstre og brødre. [Novel]. Copenhagen: Fremad, 1984.

MALINOVSKY, NINA (b. 1951)

Fri tid. [Poems]. Copenhagen: Vindrose, 1981.
Under dansens hæle. [Poems]. Copenhagen: Vindrose, 1983.
Fartens fortællinger. [Poems]. Copenhagen: Vindrose, 1985.

MARCUS, MARIA (b. 1926)

Den frygtelige sandhed. [Novel]. Copenhagen: Tiderne Skifter, 1974.

MEYER, TOVE (1913-1972)

Tiden og havet: digte 1935-67. [Poems]. Copenhagen: Gyldendal, 1969.

MØLLEHAVE, HERDIS (b. 1936)

Le. [Novel]. Copenhagen: Lindhardt & Ringhof, 1977.
Lene. [Novel]. Copenhagen: Lindhardt & Ringhof, 1980.
Helene. [Novel]. Copenhagen: Lindhardt & Ringhof, 1983.

MØRCH, DEA TRIER, see Trier Mørch, Dea.

NAGEL, ESTER (b. 1918)

Havets døtre i vinden og andre noveller. [Short stories]. Copenhagen: Gyldendal, 1976.

PREISLER, JULIANE, see p. 153

RISBJERG THOMSEN, GRETHE (b. 1925)

Udvalgte digte 1945-64. [Poems]. Copenhagen: Hasselbach, 1966.

RYUM, ULLA (b. 1937)

Natsangersken. [Novel]. Fredensborg: Arena, 1963.
Tusindskove: hændelser og historier. [Short stories]. Copenhagen: Gyldendal, 1969.
Noter om idag og igår: nye og gamle historier. [Short stories]. Copenhagen: Gyldendal, 1971.*
Myterne: menneskespil i 1 akt for 9 levende. [Play]. Copenhagen: Drama, 1975.
Baglandstekster. [Novel]. Copenhagen: Brøndum, 1983.

*Published in English:

The Siamese Cat. Tr. Paula Hostrup-Jessen. Short story from this collection in: *The Devil's Instrument and Other Danish Stories.* London: Peter Owen, 1971.

STENBÆK JENSEN, GRETE (b. 1925)

Indimellem holder de af hinanden. [Novel]. Copenhagen: Borgen, 1969.
Gade op og gade ned. [Novel]. Copenhagen: Borgen, 1973.
Konen og æggene. [Novel]. Copenhagen: Gyldendal, 1973.
Brændte børn. [Poems]. Copenhagen: Borgen, 1979.
Martha! Martha!. [Novel]. Copenhagen: Gyldendal, 1980.
Lille menneske. [Novel]. Copenhagen: Borgen, 1982.
Dagen lang. [Novel]. Copenhagen: Gyldendal, 1985.

SVENDSEN, HANNE MARIE (b. 1933)

Mathildes drømmebog. [Novel]. Copenhagen: Gyldendal, 1977.
Dans under frostmånen. [Novel]. Copenhagen: Gyldendal, 1979.
Samtale med Gud og med Fandens oldemor. [Short stories]. Copenhagen: Lindhardt & Ringhof, 1982.
Guldkuglen. [Novel]. Copenhagen: Lindhardt & Ringhof, 1985.

SØRENSEN, LISE (b. 1926)

Digternes damer. [Essays]. Copenhagen: Gyldendal, 1964.
Tro dine øjne. [Poems]. Copenhagen: Gyldendal, 1973.

TAFDRUP, PIA, see p. 153

THORUP, KIRSTEN, see. p. 76

TORP, MERETE, see p. 153

TRIER MØRCH, DEA, see p. 120

VASBO, VIBEKE (b. 1944)

Al den løgn om kvindernes svaghed. [Novel]. Copenhagen: Tiderne Skifter, 1976.
Miraklet i Amalfi. [Novel]. Copenhagen: Gyldendal, 1984.

WILLUMSEN, DORRIT, see p. 102

Works about Danish Women's Literature

Brostrøm, Torben & Winge, Mette. *Danske digtere i det 20. århundrede*, 1-5. [Articles with biographical notes]. Copenhagen: G.E.C. Gads Forlag, 1980.

Dalager, Stig & Mai, Anne Marie. *Danske kvindelige forfattere.* [Literary history] 1-2. Copenhagen: Gyldendal, 1982.

Koch, Nynne & Winther, Annie. *Kvindeforskning. Women's Studies.* [Bibliography with English summaries]. Copenhagen: Det Kongelige Bibliotek, 1981.

Levy, Jette Lundbo. *De knuste spejle: billeder og modbilleder i kvindelitteratur.* [Essays]. Copenhagen: Tiderne Skifter, 1976.

Richard, Anne Birgitte. *Kvindeoffentlighed 1968-75. Om kvindelitteratur og kvindebevægelse i Danmark.* [Essays]. Copenhagen: Gyldendal, 1978.

Roxmann, Susanna. *Kvindelige forfattere: kvinders litteraturhistorie fra antikken til vore dage.* [Literary history]. Copenhagen: Blytmann, 1985.

Bibliography

Dania Polyglotta. Literature on Denmark in languages other than Danish, and books of Danish interest published abroad. Compiled by the Danish Department of the Royal Library. Copenhagen: The Royal Library, New series 1970- [Annual].

Schroeder, Carol L. *A Bibliography of Danish Literature in English Translation 1950-1980 with a Selection of Books about Denmark.* Copenhagen: Det danske Selskab, 1982.

INDEX

Unless otherwise stated references are to Danish authors (except those mentioned in the bibliography only).

Abildgaard, Nicolai (1743-1809), Danish painter, 132

Andersen, Vita (b. 1944), 140

Andrézel, Pierre, pseudonym of Karen Blixen, 12

Antonioni, Michelangelo (b. 1912), Italian film director, 68

Aquinas, Saint Thomas of (1225-74), Italian theologian and philosopher, 44

Assisi, Saint Francis of (1182-1226), founder of the Franciscans and principal patron of Italy, 30, 44

Baggesen, Jens (1764-1826), 108

Balzac, Honoré de (1799-1850), French writer, 69

Bech, Bodil (1889-1942), 139

Beckett, Samuel (b. 1906), Irish-French writer, 67

Begtrup, Holger (1859-1937), Danish folk high school principal, 50

Blixen, Karen (1885-1962), 9-23, 25-44, 45-56, 85, 100, 107

Blixen-Finecke, Bror von (1886-1946), Swedish baron, 12, 15, 17

Brandes, Georg (1842-1927), 19

Bronzino, Angelo (1503-72), Italian painter, 51

Brøgger, Suzanne (b. 1944), 77-88, 93, 94, 95

Burchardt, Jakob (1818-97), Swiss art historian and historian of civilisation, 51

Byron, George Gordon Lord (1788-1824), British poet, 132

Bønnelycke, Emil (1893-1953), 139

Chomsky, Noam (b. 1928), American linguist, 138

Christensen, Inger (b. 1935), 65, 135-138, 140-148, 151

Claussen, Sophus (1865-1931), 28

Dante, Alighieri (1265-1321), Italian poet, 146

Descartes, René (1596-1650), French philosopher and mathematician, 147

Dinesen, Isak, see Blixen, Karen

Dinesen, Thomas (1892-1979), Danish civil engineer and writer, 16, 20

Ditlevsen, Tove (1917-76), 139, 140

Drachmann, Holger (1846-1908), 14

Engels, Friedrich (1820-95), German-Polish socialistic theorist and politician, 112

Fibonacci, Leonardo (1170-1230), Italian mathematician, 143

Finch Hatton, Denys (1887-1931), English officer, trader and safari leader, 18, 19, 20

Freud, Sigmund (1856-1939), Austrian psychoanalyst, 48, 127

Gaulle, Charles de (1890-1970), French general and politician, 107

Goethe, Johann Wolfgang von (1749-1832), German poet, 36, 49, 54

Gress, Elsa (b. 1919), 121-133

Grundtvig, N. F. S. (1783-1872), Danish clergyman, historian and poet, 119

Hamsun, Knut (1859-1952), Norwegian writer, 63, 64

Hansen, Martin A. (1909-55), 49

Hatton, Denys Finch, see Finch Hatton, Denys

Henning Jensen, Astrid (b. 1914), Danish film director, 114

Henningsen, Poul (1894-1967), Danish architect, writer and critic, 130

Hertel, Hans (b. 1939), Danish literary historian, 129

Holstein, Ludvig (1864-1943), 19

Jacobsen, Egill (b. 1910), Danish painter, 110

Jensen, Astrid Henning, see Henning Jensen, Astrid

Kafka, Franz (1883-1924), Austrian writer, 63, 64, 67

Keats, John (1795-1821), British poet, 42

Kierkegaard, Søren (1813-55), Danish philosopher and writer, 63, 64

Kistrup, Jens (b. 1925), Danish literary critic, 116

Knudsen, Jakob (1858-1917), 50

Kristensen, Tom (1893-1974), 108

Laing, R. D. (b. 1927), Scottish psychiatrist, 65

Lenin, Vladimir Ilyich (1870-1924), Soviet-Russian politician, 51

Lessing, Doris (b. 1919), British writer, 49

Lévi-Strauss, Claude (b. 1908), French social anthropologist, 147

Majakovskij, Vladimir (1893-1930), Soviet poet and playwright, 112

Malinowski, Ivan (b. 1926), 109, 112

Mantegna, Andrea (1431-1506), Italian painter, 143

Marx, Karl (1818-83), German philosopher, 48, 112

Maupassant, Guy de (1850-93), French writer, 53

McCarthy, Mary (b. 1912), American writer and critic, 129

Michaux, Henri (b. 1899), French writer and painter, 68

Miller, Henry (1891-1980), American writer, 80

Mozart, Wolfgang Amadeus (1756-91), Austrian composer, 52

Murdoch, Iris (b. 1919), British writer, 49

Mørch, Dea Trier, see Trier Mørch, Dea

Mørch, Ibi Trier, see Trier Mørch, Ibi

Nabokov, Vladimir (1899-1977), Russian-American writer, 67

Neruda, Pablo (1904-73), Chilean poet, 112

Nielsen, Hans-Jørgen (b. 1941), 107

Norén, Lars (b. 1944), Swedish writer, 68

O'Horgan, Tom (b. 1924), American stage director, 131, 132

Paludan, Jacob (1896-1975), 130

Pinter, Harold (b. 1930), British playwright, 70

Preisler, Juliane (b. 1959), 150-151

Rifbjerg, Klaus (b. 1931), 107, 108

Rilke, Rainer Maria (1875-1926), Austrian poet, 33

Rousseau, Jean-Jacques (1712-78), French writer and philosopher, 53

Schade, Jens August (1903-78), 139

Scherfig, Hans (1905-79), 108

Shakespeare, William (1564-1616), British poet, 36

Skram, Amalie (1846-1905), Norwegian writer, 70

Strandgaard, Charlotte (b. 1943), 65

Svevo, Italo (1861-1928), Italian wri-
    ter, 63, 64

Tafdrup, Pia (b. 1952), 149-150
Thorup, Kirsten (b. 1942), 59-76, 148
Torp, Merete (b. 1956), 152
Trakl, Georg (1877-1914), Austrian
    poet, 112
Trier, Ernst (1837-93), Danish folk
    high school principal, 109
Trier, Troels (b. 1940), Danish painter
    and musician, 113
Trier Mørch, Dea (b. 1941), 103-120
Trier Mørch, Ibi (Elisabeth) (1910-
    80), Danish architect, 109

Tussaud, Marie (1760-1850), French,
    founder of Madame Tussaud's wax-
    work exhibition, 99

Willumsen, Dorrit (b. 1940), 65, 66,
    89-101, 148
Wivel, Ole (b. 1921), Danish publish-
    er and poet, 49, 55
Wright, Clifford (b. 1919), American
    painter, 125

Ørnsbo, Jess (b. 1932), 94

DET DANSKE SELSKAB

The Danish Cultural Institute (*Det danske Selskab*) is an independent, non-profit institution under the Danish Ministry of Cultural Affairs. It receives an annual government grant.

The aim of the Institute is to inform about Danish life and thought and to promote cultural co-operation with other peoples. The Institute tries to obtain this aim through summer schools, educational courses, exhibitions, lectures, teaching of Danish, concert arrangements, the publication of books, etc.

The Institute has a number of cultural institutes abroad, in Austria (Salzburg), Benelux (Brussels), France (Rouen), Great Britain (Edinburgh), Italy (Milan), and West Germany (Dortmund). All institutes have libraries and other information material and function as centres for all-round information about Danish society and culture.

A wide range of Institute publications are available in English. The following books related to the subject of this book were published:

Borum, Poul. *Danish Literature – A Short Critical Survey*. 1979.
Dahlsgård, Inger. *Women in Denmark – Yesterday and Today*. 1980.